The Eternal

Science of Sanătan Philosophy

The Eternal

Science of Sanătan Philosophy

PRAKRITI PRASANNA OJHA

Bigfoot Publications
Because, there's a writer in everyone.

The Eternal : Science of Sanãtan Philosophy
Author : Prakriti Prasanna Ojha

First Published by
Bigfoot06 Publications (OPC) Pvt. Ltd.
1st floor, BSR Building near Vishal Mega Mart,
Daultabad Flyover, Laxman Vihar Phase 3,
Gurugram, Haryana (122001)
Website: www.bigfootpublications.in
Email: info@bigfootpublications.in

First Edition : September, 2023

ISBN Print Book - **978-81-19512-27-0**

Printed in India

DEDICATION

This book is dedicated to my parents-my first Gurus, who provided me with suitable and pious environment for my mental and spiritual elevation.

FOREWORD

This book, "The Eternal: Science of Sanãtan Philosophy," weaves a garland of ethical and scientific pearls of austerity into the sacred life of mankind. It resides at the cusp of transcendental and non-transcendental behaviors of nature and all forms of life. This book presents a novel exploration of the attributes of *Sanãtan Dharma* in the context of today's science. The scientific aspects of Sanãtan Dharma are eloquently elucidated through the "human-nature" relationship and in chronological order. The implications of the subtle body's connection to its transcendental manifestation and vice-versa through penance, yoga, and spiritual practices, as undergone by *Rishis*, *Munis*, and Seers, are illuminated in this work. The impacts and efficacy of these practices, and how they are intertwined with space, time, and the harmony of nature, are beautifully described.

Going through the book, it is easily conceived that *Sanãtan Dharma* is the mother of modern science. Modern science is derived from it and its insistence on energy in wave form is the root cause of the entire creation. This idea is the catalyst for the recent costly experiment of world scientists at CERN in the "Proton Proton Collider."

The freedom of arguments, crisp comments are invited with a great deal of passion by the founders of *Sanãtan Dharma: Rishis, Munis*, and Seers. This dialectic approach caused followers of *Sanãtan Dharma*, called Hindus, to be accommodative, inclusive, and submissive to other religions, sects, and cults. The pluralistic legacy is still instilled in all growing children of Hindus from birth. In contrast, other religions are rigidly bound by certain orders and commandments. Doubts and discussions are forbidden there.

The author says that in science, there are many variables depending on constraints and conditions of experiments. But while measuring one invariant from different reference frames, not only parameters but also their values are changed.

Contrastingly, in *Sanãtan Dharma*, there is only one invariant: Truth (God, *Ishvar*). Here also, parameters are different for different *Panths* (sects). Just as elements of metric transformation depend on the frame of reference in science, the thoughts and rituals of *Panths* (sects) change.

It is advised that every inquisitive mind, especially youths, should study the text of the book to dispel doubts, for spiritual awakening, and to grasp the important scientific and logical facts of the great *Sanãtan* philosophy.

Again, I agree with the author's view that without knowledge of the lexicon of *Sanãtan Dharma*, any comment or criticism is not genuinely informed. In the absence of knowledge of the lexicon and their meanings in that particular context of discussion, such comments remain a pseudo-discussion between two pseudo-scholars.

The author excels in explaining the sermons given in *Vedas, Upanishads, Gitã, Brahmasutra, Yogsutra*, and the six schools of Indian philosophy in chronological order and their repetitions time and again in these scriptures and epics. This shows that these sermons are eternal and timeless. The in-depth explanation of the attributes of science by *Sanãtan Dharma* is an excellent creation of the author.

This book is a cresset for the digressed humanity bewildering in darkness, seeking peace and harmony in human life with a serene soul. The author will be remembered for a long time for carving a new dimension in book writing.

Dr N. R. Lall,
Former Professor in Physics,
Dean (Academics)
NIT Patna

CONTENTS

INTRODUCTION

In this age of science and mass communication, everyone seeks knowledge based on logic. Science and philosophy both strive to uncover truth, yet their methods differ significantly, each with its own distinct field of study. *Sanătan Dharma* shares a similarity with science in that both encourage doubts, arguments, and reasoning. This uniqueness of *Sanătan Dharma* is scarcely found in other religions, rendering its philosophical aspect logical, reasonable, and closely aligned with modern science.

However, a facet of the *Dharma* known as *Pară Vidyă* or transcendental knowledge cannot be attained through mere reasoning.

Within this book, I endeavor to present logical and spiritual aspects of Indian philosophy. The parallels between science and philosophy foster clarity and faith, crucial in our times.

It's commonly perceived that *Sanătan Dharma* is a complex religion, with numerous scriptures and thinkers. Yet, a deeper exploration reveals interconnected paths leading to a shared destination of spirituality, morality, and universal harmony, transcending class or community.

Admittedly, comprehending the philosophical component of *Sanătan Dharma* isn't easy for everyone. Fortunately, multiple paths exist, and individuals are free to select a path or combination thereof that resonates with their interests and depth of understanding.

Thousands of years ago, when much of the world languished in ignorance, *Rishis* reveled in profound philosophy, the beauty of nature, poetry, devotion, and emotion.

Sanătan Dharma is the outcome of tireless and focused efforts by *Rishis*, who honed their insight in the seclusion of forests, deeply studying nature and revealing truths. Morally upright and spiritually elevated, *Rishis* were always eager to contribute to the establishment of universal humanism.

Every learned individual should possess a curiosity to grasp, at the very least, a general understanding of the wisdom imparted by our ancient *Rishis*, wisdom that has garnered appreciation even from renowned Western thinkers. In this book, readers will encounter significant quotations from revered Scriptures of *Sanătan Dharma*, such as *Vedas*, *Upanishads*, *Bhagavad - Gită*, and *Brahmasutra*, alongside the scientific perspectives of the six schools of Indian philosophy established by ancient Rishis.

This book caters especially to the youth. Present-day youths are more educated, skilled, and studious, yet they possess limited insight into the core of *Sanătan* philosophy. With a logical intellect and a penchant for English-language reading, I have culled logical and scientific facts predominantly from authoritative scriptures of *Sanătan Darshan*.

Within this *Dharma*, all are free to voice their opinions. Regrettably, some Hindus, due to lack of knowledge, critique this great *Dharma*. In light of this, I also delve into criticisms of *Sanătan Dharma*.

I would find great joy if this book is well-received and studied. I am confident that upon reading it, you will gain an overview of many significant scientific facts and popular quotations from *Sanătan* literature, which can facilitate spiritual awakening.

I express deep gratitude to my parents and my wife for fostering a religious and virtuous environment within our family. This environment motivated and inspired my pursuit of philosophy, even as a science student. I am appreciative of my children – Bharti, Puneet, and Suman – as well as my granddaughter Myra, for their assistance and encouragement in my endeavor to write this book.

Prakriti Prasanna Ojha

CHAPTER : 1
ABOUT SANĂTAN DHARMA

- *"There is no book in the world that is so thrilling, stirring and inspiring as the Upanishads."*

  -Max Muller, a famous German philologist

- *"India is, the cradle of human race, the birthplace of human speech, the mother of history, the grand mother of legend, and the great grand mother of tradition. Our most valuable and most constructive materials in the history of man are treasured up in India only."*

  -Mark Twain, a famous American author

- *"If there is one place on the face of the earth where all the dreams of living men have found a home from the very earliest days when man began the dream of existence, it is India."*

  -Romain Rolland, a French writer and novelist

- *"India is the mother of our race and Sanskrit the mother of our philosophy, mother through the Arabs, of much of our Mathematics, mother through Buddha, of the idea embodied in Christianity, mother through the village community of self-government and democracy. Mother India in many ways is the mother of us all."*

-Will Durant, a famous American writer & historian,

in his book 'Our Oriental Heritage'

Sanătan Dharma is the knowledge gathered by many *Rishis*, seers, and thinkers from time immemorial. *Sanătan* means eternal, with no beginning and end. We may say that there is no point of origin of *Sanătan Dharma*.

One can see the *Richa* of stone age in *Rigveda* :

जरतीभिः औषधिभिः पर्णेभिः शकुनानाम् ।
कार्मारो अश्मभिः द्युभिः हिरण्यवन्तम् इच्छति । ऋगवेद 9.112.2

(The artisan, who prepares medicine and makes arrows from feathers and sharp stones, wishes for rich persons to buy their goods.)

This *Dharma* has no end point. It is not a closed religion. Its doors are always open for excellence.

A *Richa* from the *Rigveda*, the oldest available literature in the world, states:

आ नो भद्राः क्रतवो यन्तु विश्वतो अदब्धासो अपरितास उद्भिदः ।
देवा नो यथासदभिद् वृधे असन्नाप्रायुवो रक्षितोरो दिवे दिवे ।
ऋग्वेद. 89 .देवता- विश्वदेवाः

(May noble and sublime thoughts come to us from all directions, taking us to a higher level. May the gods, who protect us and increase our progress, be with us day after day.)

Sanătan Dharma is the spontaneous flow of feelings and thoughts of *Rishis*. It is not a certain cult or prescribed path; it is universal. It has an all-embracing vision and is loaded with love and thoughts of collective welfare for all beings.

Religion is not synonymous with *Dharma*. *Dharma* is not a specific path or stream; it is an ocean where streams merge while still maintaining their identity.

The objective of *Dharma* is peace, well-being, and a settled order for all beings in the world. *Sanătan Dharma* has no single founder; it has gradually flourished through evolution, resulting from the efforts, analysis, and intuitive revelations of many *Rishis* over thousands of years.

Just as science is developed and confirmed through regular experiments, analysis, and discussions, much of the knowledge in the authoritative texts of *Dharma* has been derived from practical experience, analysis, perception, the quest for truth and wisdom, discussion, vision, inner quest, contemplation, and combinations of the above, carried out by our *Rishis* over thousands of years. The *Rishis* devoted selfless work in the right direction and spirit to make the world a better place to live. Many of them lived in the solitude of the forest, considered suitable for the growth of insight and inner quest.

The purpose of *Dharma* can be best understood through the popular lines of *Brihadăranyaka Upanishad:*

असतो मा सद्गमय, तमसो मा ज्योतिर्गमय, मृत्योर्मा अमृत गमय।

(Let us move from fallacy to truth, from darkness to light, from mortality to immortality.)

The *Rigveda* states:

उदीर्ध्वम् जीवो असुः नः प्रागात् तमः आ ज्योतिः एति। ऋग्वेद 1.113.16

(Wake up; the light, which is our life, has come.)

Light represents sacredness, purity, enlightenment, wisdom, and truth, while darkness symbolizes evil, ignorance, and illusion.

The great scientist Einstein remarked: "The more I study science, the more I believe in God."

Both science and *Dharma* are in search of truth. Hindu philosophy is logical like science, very liberal, and sophisticated. However, there are some aspects of philosophy that cannot be achieved through reasoning.

न एषा तर्केण मतिः आपनेया । कठोपनिषद 1.9

(This truth cannot be achieved by reasoning.)

Upanishads categorize knowledge into two parts - परा (transcendental) and अपरा (non-transcendental). Transcendental knowledge is revealed through vision, insight, intuition, and experience. Non-transcendental knowledge is the knowledge of reason, but transcendental knowledge cannot be achieved by reasoning alone. As for Pară *Vidyă*, the scriptures define:

अथ परा यया तत् अक्षरम् अधिगम्यते । मुण्डकोपनिषद 1.1.5

(Through *Pară Vidyă*, the Imperishable is realised.)

Rationality is also of prime importance among all the six schools of Indian philosophy.

Upanishads are the most revered scriptures for Hindus. They are the essence and explanation of *Vedas*, and thus they are also called *Vedăntas*. *Bhagvad Gită* is the essence of *Upanishads* and has become the most popular philosophical scripture not only among Hindus but also around the world.

Upanishads are full of wisdom, aiming for the welfare of the entire creation. They are based on the great theory of 'microcosm is macrocosm'.

अहम् ब्रह्मास्मि। तत् त्वम् असि ।

("I am *Brahman*, God, and the same are you.")

What a great statement, also supported by the statements in *Upanishads*.

ईशा वास्यमिदम् सर्वम् यदकिंचित जगत्यां जगत्। ईशावास्योपनिषद मंत्र 1

("God or Super Conscious pervades the entire universe, whatsoever.")

Every being is like a wave in the ocean, which maintains its individuality due to its shape and temporary life, but it is not separate from the ocean. These statements from the *Upanishads* are so profound that they explain both philosophical and scientific theories. This view of the *Upanishads* provides a solution to environmental problems. These lofty thoughts are also coherent with the Quantum Theory of modern science, which will be discussed in detail later on.

Religion is not the exact translation of *Dharma*. There is no proper equivalent word in English for the term *Dharma*. It is a *Sanskrit* word that originates from the root *'Dhri,'* which means 'to hold, support, or sustain,' holding virtues and righteousness for the collective welfare of the entire creation. Therefore, *Dharma* can be called the universal religion.

Darshan arises from the *Sanskrit* root *'Dri,'* which means 'to see,' and that is why the *Rishis* are called seers. It also includes inner quest, inner vision, or insight. The concept of *Dharma* is based on the idea that the universe is governed by a law called *Rit* (ऋत्), and *Dharma* should be in agreement with that cosmic law. *Dharma* refers to the proper and ideal conduct of people to suit the goal of life and the collective welfare of all. Hinduism has many thinkers, seers, and sacred books, but Vedas, *Upanishads*, *Gită*, *Brahmasutra*, and *Yogasutra* of *Patanjali* are considered authoritative for arguments, and generally quotations were cited from these books during philosophical discussions. These scriptures are both logical and authentic sources of transcendental and non-transcendental knowledge.

Due to the freedom of opinion and reason, several sects and paths were developed, but each one respects the others and are interconnected. One is free to choose any one or any combination of sects or paths that suit them.

At the time of *Buddha*, there were more than seventy sects of Hinduism in India. The main points of differences and discussions were about the Ultimate truth (God) and the start of the universe (transcendental knowledge, परा ज्ञान). Like many other thinkers, *Buddha* was not satisfied with this situation. If we have no complete knowledge of the creation, that is the universe, how can we expect to know the creator, and if we don't have complete knowledge, how can we discuss it.

अचिंत्यं चिंत्यमानः अपि चिन्तारूपं भजत्यसौ । अष्टावक्र गीता 12.7

(It is futile to think about matters beyond knowledge and conception of the mind.)

Buddha thought that life is short, and these discussions are futile, nothing but a wastage of valuable time in human life. That's why he came out in search of a performance-based principle and path for the welfare of humanity, and freedom from the bondage of the life-cycle, which is the cause of suffering.

When I talk about *Sanătan Dharma*, I also include *Buddhism*, *Jainism*, *Sikhism*, and all six schools of *Indian* philosophy because they are sects of *Sanătan Dharma*, which have flourished and developed in the same light and environment. It is also called *Dharma* in *Jainism* and *Dhamma* in *Buddhism*.

Hindus have great reverence for the founders and preachers of the above *Dharmas*. They worship *Buddha* and *Rishabh Deva*, the founder of *Jainism*, as the incarnation of *Lord Vishnu*. Consciously or unconsciously, Hindus were influenced by *Jainism* and *Buddhism*. They absorbed the best elements of the above philosophies, such as controlling animal sacrifice. Hindus also respect *Bhagavăn Mahăvir*, a great *Muni* of *Jainism*, and *Guru Nănakadev*, the founder of *Sikhism*.

Both *Buddha* and *Patanjali* were influenced by *Maharshi Kapil*, the founder of the *Sămkhya Darshan*. *Kapila Muni* is a great philosopher of antiquity, and his name appears in *Rigveda*, *Upanishads*, and the *Bhagvad Gită*.

The importance of *Kapil* can be understood from the fact that in the *Bhagvad Gită*, *Lord Krishna* says: 'सिद्धानां कपिलो मुनिः' (I am *Kapila Muni* among the perfect ones). *Lord Krishna* intends to say that *Maharshi Kapil* is the greatest among the seers. *Sămkhya Darshan* is one of the oldest schools of Indian philosophy, founded by *Maharshi Kapila*.

'ऋषिं प्रसूतं यस्तमग्रे ज्ञानैः विभातिं याजमानम् च पश्येत् ।
Shvetashvatar Upanishad 5.2

(*Kapila* is among the first who has seen the growth of illuminating wisdom.)

Most of the basic principles of *Buddhism* were influenced by *Kapila's Sămkhya Darshan*. Both consider God as an unnecessary postulate. *Sămkhya* and *Buddhism* never argue for the non-existence of God.

It should be noted that *Buddhism* and *Jainism* are not atheist philosophies, as supposed by some persons. *Bhagavăn Buddha* used to say: everything is under flames of fire, we should discuss only essential and useful matters.

In *Jătak Kathă*, *Buddha* indirectly expressed that life is short and it is useless to discuss the inconceivable. The story goes like this: When *Buddha* was sitting with a close follower, the follower inquired him: "You are enlightened, but you keep mum when asked about God?" As an answer, Buddha told a story instead of a direct answer:

'Two friends were passing through a lonely jungle when a random arrow wounded the arm of a friend, and it started to bleed. The other friend wanted to treat the wound immediately to stop the bleeding, but the wounded friend refused to cooperate. He asked, "First of all, explain who has shot the arrow? What's the reason? Who is our enemy in this lonely forest? Is this arrow poisonous?" In this way, he raised a number of questions. The other friend answered, "Your arm is bleeding profusely. The time is less. The delay may be dangerous. It may be fatal."

With the help of the story, *Buddha* intended to communicate that life is short and the journey to get rid of the bondage of death is long. We should not waste our precious time in discussions of no use at this stage. *Buddha* avoided arguments about the creator or creation of the universe, when more than 75 sects of Hindus were busy mainly in these arguments.

Jainism, which has faith in personal soul, cannot deny the existence of the Super Soul, which is the ultimate goal of *Jains'* journey of life. Jainism has faith in the individual soul with infinite potential.

Buddha was born and brought up in *Kapilavastu*, where the *Sămkhya Darshan* was dominant, and his childhood teachers were followers of *Sămkhya. Alăra Kalăma* of *Vaishăli*, the first preacher of *Buddha*, was also a follower of *Sămkhya.*

"Jainism and Buddhism, both derived their basic principles from the Upanishads, although they denied the authenticity of Vedas as an infalliable authority and the efficacy of rites prescribed in them, both ignored the idea of God."

- 'Ancient India' by R.C. Majumdar

Jainism is a very ancient religion, and *Mahăvir* is the 24th *Tirthankar* of the religion. *Tirthankars* were not in continuous succession. The 22nd *Tirthankar*, *Aristnemi*, is considered contemporary to and a cousin brother of *Lord Krishna.* This allows us to estimate the period of the first *Tirthankar* and founder of *Jainism*, *Rishabhadeva* (ऋषभदेव), whose name appears in the Rigveda, the oldest literature in the world. According to the *Bhagavat Purăna*, *Rishabhadeva* is respected as one of the 24 *Avatărs* of *Vishnu*. *Bhagavăn Mahăvir* is the last of the long series of illustrious preachers. *Părsvanath* and *Mahăvir* are widely known preachers of *Jainism.* All the *Tirthankars* are respected by Hindus. *Bhagavăn Buddha* is also revered as one of the ten incarnations of *Vishnu*. *Adishankărachărya*, a famous monastic *saint* of Hindus, who is also known for his arguments against *Buddhism*, has written prayers for *Buddha* and honoured him. *Guru Nănakadev*, the founder of *Sikhism*, is also respected by Hindus. Hindu philosophies keep evolving and are always open to accepting and transforming ideas.

CHAPTER : 2

FREEDOM TO DOUBT, ARGUE AND DISCUSS

Billions of years ago, after the appearance of living beings on Earth, the process of evolution started and continues to this day. Doubts, questions, and logic are potent factors for evolution, and *Sanătan Dharma* encourages them. Unlike some other religions, *Sanătan* philosophy does not rely on blind faith. Any matter or knowledge can be considered scientific if it is logical. There should be freedom to raise doubts and ask questions, as they are the mother of science and philosophy. Philosophy is the love for wisdom, and arguments are essential for any matter of universal character.

Like science, *Sanătan Dharma* has a universal character. Anyone is free to raise doubts or ask questions. The *Dharma* is meant for all, for the betterment of all, not just a specific group of people. Despite having numerous scriptures and thinkers, Sanătan Dharma remains open to learning more.

उत्तिष्ठ जाग्रत प्राप्य वरान् निबोधत... कठोपनिषद 1/3/14

(Rise, awake and receive which is more sublime)

Any question can be asked from the philosophical aspects of the *Dharma*. However, for transcendental knowledge, one must approach an able *Guru*. In the *Bhagvad Gită*, *Lord Krishna* advises to go to a knowledgeable person, bow before him, and ask questions with good intentions.

तद्विद्धि प्रणिपातेन परिप्रश्नेन सेवया,
उपदेक्ष्यन्ति ते ज्ञानं ज्ञानिनस्तत्वदर्शिनः। गीता 4.34

(Try to learn the truth by approaching the spiritual master. Inquire from him submissively and render service unto them. The self-realised souls can impart knowledge unto you because they have seen the truth.)

Teachings of the *Upanishads* are, generally, in a question-answer format. Disciples are free to ask questions to their *Gurus*. In *Kathopanishad*, a curious child named *Nachiketa* asks questions to *Yama*, the god of death, to know about transcendental knowledge. In the *Bhagvad Gită*, *Arjuna* not only listens to the advice of *Lord Krishna* but also asks questions to clear his doubts.

Rabindranath Tagore expressed his values and wishes clearly in *Gitănjali*:

"Where the mind is without fear and the head is held high; Where knowledge is free;... Where the clear stream of reason has not lost its way into the dreary desert sand of dead habits;... Into the heaven of freedom, my Father, let my country awake."

In ancient India, philosophical and intellectual debates called *Shastrarth* were prevalent, where scholars were free to argue and discuss the inner meaning of life and Hindu scriptures. Generally, in other religions, individuals who doubt established beliefs are punished. But in *Sanătan Dharma*, even famous atheists like *chărvăka* are respected as thinkers. In the *Nyăy* system of Indian philosophy, doubt (*Sanshaya*), argumentation (*Tarka*), and discussion (*Văda*) are acknowledged as means of true knowledge.

Even in the *Rigveda*, the *Rishis* have frankly admitted that they are doubtful about the full knowledge of the creation and creator of the Universe. In one hymn, the *Rishi* states that the world arose from *Tapas*, and then admits that he is not sure of this hypothesis, and suggests that even the highest god *Prajăpati* may not know the truth.

In another hymn, the *Rishi* states, 'He from whom all this creation came, whether He created or... The highest Seer that is in the highest heaven, He knows it, or perhaps even He knows not.' (*Rigved* 10.129, Translated by Max Muller)

This is perhaps the first philosophical doubt in world literature. Some Upanishads also criticized the rituals (कर्म कांड) advocated by the Vedas. In *Mandukya Upanishad*, rituals have been compared to a broken boat (to cross the ocean of delusion).

In the *Bhagvad Gită*, *Lord Krishna* suggests:

त्रैगुण्यविषया वेदा निस्त्रैगुण्यो भवार्जुन । 2.45

(*Vedas* deal with matters related to the three *Gunas* (*Sat*, *Raj*, *Tam*) but *Arjuna*! You have to be free from these *Gunas*.)

Everyone is free to doubt and argue and choose their own option among the several paths (*Panths*). Every individual can have direct communication with God in their own way, no mediator is essential between man and God. This Dharma respects an individual's freedom of thoughts. This is the beauty of *Sanătan Dharma*.

Indian philosophy is so rich that it influenced the entire world, and thinkers all over the world appreciated its depth. Western philosophy was influenced by Indian philosophy. Plato, a famous philosopher of ancient Greece, the founder of the first institute of higher learning in the western world, was also influenced by Indian philosophy. After the persecution of Socrates (399 B.C.), his nearest follower Plato realised that Athens was not safe for him and in the same year 399 B.C., he set out and wandered for 12 years from Egypt to India, imbibing wisdom from every source. During this period, he found his way to the bank of the river Ganges in India and learned a lot from Hindus. *(Source: 'The Story of Philosophy' by Will Durant)*

Schopenhauer, a famous Western philosopher of the 19th century, writes: "The Hindus were deeper than the thinkers of Europe because their interpretation of the world was internal and intuitive, not external and intellectual; the intellect divides everything, intuition unites everything... '*That art thou.*' Whoever is able to say this to himself, with regard to every being with whom he comes in contact, is clear-eyed and clear-souled enough to see that we are all members of one organism, all of us little currents in an ocean of will; he is certain of all virtues and blessedness and is on the direct road to salvation."

Again he writes that Indian philosophy streamed into Europe and would profoundly alter our knowledge and our thought.

Even Persian mysticism borrowed heavily from *Upanishads*. *Ghălib* writes:

'इशरते कतरा है दरिया में फना हो जाना'

(The glory of the drop is to merge itself in the vastness of the river).

Mansur Al-Hallăj (858-922 C.E.), a Persian poet and teacher of *Sufism*, set out on a long voyage that took him to India. He was deeply influenced by *Upanishads*. He is famous for his saying - *'Ana'l-Haqq'* (I am truth), which is the same as 'अहम् ब्रह्मास्मि' of *Upanishad*. *Sufi* poet *Iqbăl* writes - "बस नाम रहेगा अल्लाह का, जो मैं भी हूँ और तुम भी हो।" The above statement is not different from 'अहम् ब्रह्मास्मि' of *BrihaDărănyak Upanishad* and 'तत् त्वम असि' of *Chhandogya Upanishad.*

Other religions show the path, but *Sanătan Dharma* shows the direction with several paths to choose from or suitable combinations, whichever suits. There is a difference of opinion among the *Rishis*, which is natural where there is freedom of opinion. In spite of the differences, all *Rishis* and thinkers are respected. There are a number of sects, and every sect wants to establish its supremacy, but only by philosophical arguments called shătrărth. Every Hindu has respect for all thinkers, whatever may be their faith. Adi *Shankar*, *Rămanujăchărya*, *Guru Nănak*, *Guru Gorakhanath*, *Swami RamĂnand*, *Kabir*, *Tulsi*, *Raidăs*, *Buddha*, *Mahăvir* all are respected. They have some different opinions but with one commonality, that is the happiness and peace of all and to preach unto mankind their divinity.

In *Sanătan Dharma*, the Rishis are not the messengers of God but they are *Drasta* (द्रष्टा), seers with logic and insight both. The basic word for Drashta and Darshan is *'Drish* (दृश्)' which means 'to see,' to see inward and outward, to have wisdom by insight or external experiences.

ऋषयः मंत्रद्रष्टारः ।

(*Rishis* are the seers of *Mantras*)

The truth was revealed to many *Rishis*, so no one claims to be the founder of the *Dharma*. Ultimate truth or transcendental knowledge (परा विद्या) cannot be understood by erudition only.

ध्याननिर्मथना अभ्यासात् देवं पश्येत् निगूढ़वत् ।

Shvetashvatar Upanishad 1.14

(Through the practice of churning by *Dhyăna*, *Devas* acknowledge the hidden truth.)

The more calm, serene, and free of dross the soul is, the more easily it is connected to the Cosmic Consciousness; and the truth is revealed. The ultimate truth is beyond reason. Intuitive knowledge or insight vision, which we call the sixth sense or third eye, has a vital role to play in the type of wisdom which we call *Darshan*. Some scientists have also realised this source of knowledge, sometimes in dreams, which revolutionized the scientific world. But this cannot be possible without a serene mind and cleansed soul. Intuition is the virtue of the pious soul.

यस्मिन् विशुद्धे विभाति एषः आत्मा ।

Mundakopanishad 3/1/9

(We can have glimpses of the Supreme with a pure and serene soul)

According to *Sănkhya Darshan*, the soul is the real *Drasta* or seer. *Rishis* have a calm and cleansed mind, living in solitude, beneath the trees near the rivers, and away from worldly distractions. With their serene soul, calm and collected mind, great spiritual power, and profound intuitive power, they could get glimpses of the hidden truth.

There are some differences of opinions due to the glimpses and visualizations of the truth from different frames of reference, and like the Theory of Relativity, they admit -

'एकम् सत् विप्राः बहुधा वदन्ति' ऋग्वेद 1. 164. 46

(The truth is one, which is spoken by learned persons in different ways.)

The opinions may be different, but the essence is one.

'एक वर्ण तथा दुग्धं भिन्न वर्णासु धेनुषु,
तथैव धर्म वैचित्र्ययंवमेकं परं स्मृतम्।'

Mahăbhărat

(The cows of different colours produce milk of one colour, in the same way, the essence of different religions is one.)

The purpose of these statements is to harmonize different sects and religions of the world.

'यथा नद्यः स्यन्दमानाः (बहती हुई) समुद्रे अस्तम् गच्छन्ति नामरूपे विहाय..'

(As the flowing rivers enter the ocean (truth) leaving aside their name and shape.)

Religion is not an exact synonym of *Dharma*. *Dharma* means the virtue, ideology, duty, morality, spirituality, and all the qualities a person should have for the welfare of his life and beyond, and for the happiness of the entire creation, being in tune with the creation.

In the oldest scripture of the world, the *Rigveda*, the *Rishi* desires the welfare of the world.

वैश्वानरः महिम्ना विश्वकृष्टिः।

ऋग्वेद 1.59.7

(*O Vishvănar* (Cosmic Consciousness)! Promote the welfare of the world by your glory.)

In *Sanătan Dharma*, the line that repeatedly appears in prayer is:

"तन्मे मनः शिवसंकल्पमस्तु"

(Let my mind desire welfare for all.)

The scriptures desire:

'सर्वे भवन्तु सुखिनः सर्वे सन्तु निरामयाः।

सर्वे भद्राणि पश्यन्तु मा कश्चिद् दुःख भाग्भवेत्।'

Vrihadăranyak Upanishad

(Let all be happy, let all be free from debilitation, let all see goodness, let there be no victims of sorrow.)

This is why *Sanătan Dharma* is considered a universal religion. *Dharma* may be said to be the art of living for the welfare of the maximum number. *Dharma* includes philosophy, ethics, and rituals. *Darshan* and *Dharma* have evolved gradually, and that is why it is flexible and ever-changing. It is not rigid and locked.

Sanătan scriptures advise:

उतिष्ठ जाग्रत वरान्निबोधत।

Kathopanishad

(Wake up and rise, get enlightened by the wisdom which is more sublime.)

Man, society, and the environment are always undergoing changes. It has been well said - 'You cannot bathe twice in the same river.' *Dharma* should also change accordingly, and it should be changeable. There should always be scope for some reformation. In *Sanătan Dharma*, a number of paths are available, from the worship of idols to the devotion of the formless God (*Nirăkăr Brahma*). Idol-worship is more popular among the commoners who may find it difficult to comprehend abstract and deep philosophical ideas.

Therefore, for the common people, the scriptures advise:

धर्मस्य तत्त्वं निहितं गुहायां महाजनो येन गतः सः पंथाः।

(The true nature of *Dharma* is hidden in a cave. The path is the one by which great souls travel.)

The ethics of Hindus is based on the principle of *Karma*, which means 'As you sow, so you shall reap.' Happiness and sorrow are the results of good and bad deeds done by a person in past and present lives. Hindus believe in the theory of rebirth of the soul. The theory of hell and heaven for bad and good deeds respectively is also part of the Purănas for the common people.

Despite several sects and much criticism, the percentage of atheists is relatively lower in India, the seat of *Sanătan Dharma*. In some other religions, thinkers of different ideas and opinions were humiliated, punished, and even killed. There are several examples like Socrates, Jesus, Mansur, and Bab *(Ali Mohammad Shiradi)*. Bab was the founder of Babism and a central figure of *Bahai's* Faith. He worked for the reformation of *Islam*. Socrates advocated raising questions until satisfied when there is doubt.

Hindus respect every thinker, even atheists like *Jăvăli* and *Chărvăk*. They are addressed with respect as *Munis* (thinkers). We find a reference to *Chărvăk* in the epic *Mahăbhărat*, and *Jăvăli* finds considerable space in the great epic *Rămăyăna*. *Sanătan Dharma* has a number of paths, but the objective is one, and everyone is free to choose their own path according to their interest, faith, and ability.

CHAPTER : 3
HINDU SCRIPTURES

As already mentioned, *Sanătan Dharma* has no beginning point and no one as the founder. It has a number of thinkers, *Rishis*, and philosophers. Therefore, there is a variety of scriptures and philosophies. When the rest of the world was covered with the darkness of ignorance, the *Aryans* were enjoying the bliss of philosophical depth, the beauty of nature, poetry writing, chanting *Mantras*, devotion, and emotion. Despite some of them being lost and others destroyed by invaders, there is a vast literature from ancient times.

Here is an account of some important scriptures.

Hindu scriptures are roughly divided into two classes, namely *Sruti* and *Smriti*. *Sruti* represents the revealed wisdom and higher philosophy. These were revealed by intuitive insight or Cosmic Consciousness to the *Rishis*, who are therefore called *Mantra-Drashta*, meaning "seers of the wisdom." The *Vedas* and *Upanishads* are recognised in this category and are greatly respected by Hindus and scholars worldwide. The *Bhagvad Gită* and *Brahmă Sutra*, being the essence of *Upanishads*, are also considered as Sruti. The rest are considered as Smriti, meaning "remembered."

Vedas - *Ved* means 'knowledge,' the sacred, spiritual knowledge. It is not an individual literary work but a mass of literature that has grown up over many centuries. *Vedas* are called divine because it is quite unimaginable and miraculous that thousands of years ago, when there was no printing press, thousands of *Mantras* were chanted in poetic forms, remembered, and orally handed down from generation to generation. These are the wisdom revealed to the seers called *Rishis*. *Vedas* are the oldest books in the library of humanity. They are of three classes - The *Samhitas* or *Mantras*, the *Brahmanas* and the *Ăranyakas*, and the third *Upanishads*.

The Samhită or Mantras - These are collections of hymns, prayers, chants, and sacrificial formulae. They form the oldest literary work in the world and are considered as the root of Indian philosophy, culture, and rituals.

वेदः अखिलो धर्ममूलम् । मनुस्मृति

(*Vedas* are the root of entire *Dharma* (religion))

Vedas are four in number:

1. **The Rigveda Samhită** - The word 'Rigveda' originates from the Sanskrit root *'Rik'* (ऋक्), meaning 'prayer.' *Rishis* also prayed to natural objects as the manifested Divinity. The *Rigveda Samhită* is the oldest literature of the world and has been composed according to strict metric patterns of poetry. It is a collection of 10,552 *Richas*, 1028 hymns (*Suktas*) arranged in 10 books

(*Mandals*) with extraordinary emotion, beauty, and philosophical depth.

2. **The Sămaveda Samhită** - It consists of 1810 verses, mostly borrowed from *Rigveda*, arranged according to the needs of musical notations. *Lord Krishna* himself mentions its importance in the *Bhagvad Gită*:

"वेदानाम् सामवेदः अस्मि"

गीता 10/22

(Of the Vedas, l am *Sămaveda*)

He means to say that *Sămaveda* is most respectable among the Vedas.

1. **The Yajurveda Samhită** - It deals with the details of the performance of rituals and is mostly in prose, meant to be used by priests for supplementing the Rigvedic Mantras.
2. **The Atharvaveda** - It contains hymns (some from the *Rigveda*) and deals mostly with charms, magic, and spells to win over friends, overcome demons, and gain worldly success.

The Brahmanas and the Ăranyakas - These are the prose explanations of the *Samhitas'* portions and give details and explanations of sacrificial rituals. *Ăranyakas* are written in forests and interpret sacrificial rituals in a symbolic and philosophical way.

The Upanishads - There are 108 *Upanishads*, among which nine are generally considered important. *Upanishads* contain a great variety of philosophical ideas about the universe, *Ătma* (soul), and *Brahma* (God). Even Western scholars and thinkers greatly appreciate the ancient lofty wisdom and the seers of the *Upanishads*. The most important *Upanishads* are *Ishăvasya*, *Kena*, *Katha*, *Prashna*, *Mundaka*, *Mandukya*, *Aitareya*, *Taittiriya*, and *Shvetashvatar*.

Upa-Vedas - There are four *Upa-Vedas* or subsidiary *Vedas*, namely the *Ăyurveda* (the science and art of health), the *Dhanurveda* (the science of war), the *Gandharva Veda* (the science of music), and the *Arthasastra* (the science of polity). They serve as auxiliary to the four *Vedas*.

The Vedangas - There are six *Vedangas* (limbs to the *Vedas*), namely *Shiksha* and *Vyăkarana* of *Pănini* (*Shiksha* deals with pronunciation and accent, and *Vyăkarana* is *Sanskrit* Grammar), Chhandas of *Pingalăchărya* (dealing with poetic meters and melody), *Nirukta* of *Yaska* (philology or etymology), and *Jyotisha* (astronomy and astrology, dealing with the movement of heavenly bodies and their influence on human affairs).

Kalpa - *Kalpa* is the method of rituals.

Among the *Sanătan* scriptures, *Sruti* is the primary authority while *Smriti* is secondary authority. *Smritis* are also books written by sages, but they are not the final authority. If anything in *Smriti* contradicts *Shruti*, *Shruti* will prevail. There are eighteen main *Smritis*, the most important of which are those of *Manu*, *Yăjnăvalkya*, and *Parăsara*.

The laws and rules, which are based entirely upon our social situation and time period, must change with changes in social conditions and time.

The Purănas - The *Purănas* are supposed to discuss five topics - the creation and recreation of the world, the period of various *Manus* (*manvantaras*), the genealogies of gods and *Rishis*, and the accounts of royal dynasties including the *Suryavanshi* and *Chandravanshi* kings. *Purănas* deal with these five topics and much more. The *Purănas* have accounts of mountains, rivers, and places, which are useful for the study of historical geography. Some *Purănas* also provide useful information about historical dynasties and kings. *Purănas* contain history, philosophy, ethical stories, lives of legends, kings, saints, great men, and chronicles of great historical events. The aim of *Purănas* is to impress on the minds of the masses the teachings of Vedas and to generate devotion to God. *Purănas* are meant for the common masses because Hindu *Darshans* are very stiff for a common man. The *Purănas* have a very important function as a vehicle of social and religious values. They were written to popularize the religion of the *Vedas*.

The most popular among the *Purănas* are Shrimadbhagavat and *Vishnu Purăna*, which advocate and dignify *Vaishnava Pantha*. The next one is *Shiva Purăna*, which dignifies *Shaiva Panth*, and the third one is *Markandeya Purăna*, which dignifies *Shăkta Panth*. *Markandeya Purăna* is well known for *Chandi Păth*, the prayer of Mother Durga, which is read in *Navarătri*.

The Rămăyăna and Mahăbhărat -

The *Rămăyăna*, the first epic poem, is related to the story of *Shri Răma*, the ideal man. The life of his wife *Sita* is regarded as the perfect example of womanly fidelity and sweetness. The *Rămăyăna* is written in twenty-four thousand verses by *Rishi Vălmiki* and is the oldest epic in the world. On the other hand, the *Mahăbhărat* gives the description of the great war between *Kauravas* and *Păndavas*, who were cousins and belonged to the lunar race. It is considered as the most voluminous epic in the world. Both the *Rămăyăna* and *Mahăbhărat* are magnificent epics with powerful historical stories that have captured the imagination of millions of people over the centuries. They remain popular to this day all over the world. The famous *Bhagvad Gită* is a part of the *Mahăbhărat.*

The Bhagvad Gită -

"The Bhagvad Gită is perhaps the most systematic spiritual statement of the perennial philosophy."

-Aldous Huxley, a famous English writer and philosopher

"When I read the Bhăgvad - Gită everything else seems so superfluous."

-Albert Einstein

The Gită ranks high in the religious literature of the world and is the most precious jewel of the religious literature of Hindus. The *Upanishads* explain the philosophy of the *Vedas*, and the Gită is considered the essence of the *Upanishads*. So, although the *Gită* is a part of the great epic *Mahăbhărat*, it is considered as Shruti. It is a marvelous dialogue between *Lord Krishna* and *Arjuna* on the battlefield, before the commencement of the great war of *Kurukshetra*. About the Gită, it has been well said: The *Upanishads* are the cow, *Lord Krishna* is the milkman, *Arjuna* is the calf, and the *Gită* is the milk. The wise men are those who imbibe this milk. The *Gită* is also a brilliant synthesis of different types of Yoga methods. The *Gită* is considered the most recognised and popular religious book in the world.

***Brahmasutra* -**

Sutra means a small formula. The *Brahmasutra* has been composed by *Maharshi Bădarăyan* (बादरायण). It is one of the three authoritative books of Hindus (प्रस्थान त्रयी). *Upanishads* are many in number and developed in different Vedic schools at different times and places. The problems discussed and solutions offered presented differences despite a unity of general outlook. Therefore, the need was felt for systematizing the different teachings to bring out harmony. The *Brahmasutra* undertakes this important task. The *Sutras* in the book are very short and cannot be understood without explanation. So, explanations (भाष्य) were written by great philosophers like *Shankarăchărya* and *Rămănujăchărya*.

In addition to the above scriptures, there is vast literature related to different thoughts of Indian Philosophy, such as *Nyăy*, *Vaisheshika*, *Sămkhya* , *Yoga*, *Mimănsa*, *Buddhism*, and *Jainism* developed by *Rishis* of antiquity on the Indian soil. Due to freedom of thought, there are many thinkers, and Hindus welcome all because a variety of approaches lead to the same destination.

CHAPTER : 4
CHRONOLOGY OF SCRIPTURES

Sanătana means eternal with no beginning. Most of the Scriptures are prehistoric, so there is a difference of opinion about their dates. A rough and short account is mentioned hereunder. *Vedas* are Sruti, which means they are revealed by *Rishis* in meditation and are self-existent truth. Among the scriptures, the *Rigveda Samhită* is considered the oldest. The dates suggested by different historians range from 20,000 B.C. to 800 B.C.

The controversy can be summed up by the following lines of Winternitz, an authority on the subject:

"The available evidence merely proves that the Vedic period extends from an unknown past, say X, to 500 B.C., none of the dates 1200-500 B.C., 1500-500 B.C., and 2000-500 B.C., which are usually assumed, being justified by facts. Only it may be added, as a result of recent researches, that 800 B.C. should probably be substituted for 500 B.C., and that the unknown date X more probably falls in the third rather than the second millennium before Christ."

So, the above statement shows the probability of the Vedic period being from 3000 B.C. to 800 B.C. In *Rigveda*, some hymns seem to be of the Stone Age. The Stone Age, characterized by the creation and use of stone tools, lasted up to 3300 B.C., from 2.6 million years ago. In *Rigveda*, there is a hymn that describes the preparation of arrows using dry wooden branches, bird feathers, and sharp stones (*Rigveda* - 9.112.2). There is also a description of the disappeared River *Saraswati* in *Rigveda*, which led hydrologists to calculate the beginning of the *Rigvedic* period to be around 20,000 years ago.

Max Muller, who first dealt with the question of chronology in a critical manner, stated that some of the *Upanishads* are older than *Buddha* (500 B.C.). The composition of *Purănas* started in the *Vedic* period and stretched into the 4th-5th centuries and, in some cases, even later. Actually, the exact dating of history starts after Buddha, which is the 5th century B.C. And since most of the *Sanătan* Scriptures are prehistoric, there is a difference of opinion about the dates of the scriptures. This is also the case with the great epics *Rămăyăna* and *Mahăbhărat*. According to some historians, these may have been composed around the 5th century B.C.

CHAPTER : 5

SCIENTIFIC BASIS OF KNOWLEDGE

Specially, the *Nyăy* and *Vaisheshika* schools are logical and analytic types of philosophies. Just like science, the main purpose of these two philosophies is the critical examination of the objects of knowledge by means of logical proof. According to the *Nyăy* School, the sources of knowledge are Perception (प्रत्यक्ष), Inference (अनुमान), comparison (उपमान), and testimony (शब्द). The Nyăy is a work of the great sage *Gautam*, estimated to be from around the 6th century BCE.

Patanjali, the founder of the Yoga system, also says:

'प्रत्यक्ष अनुमान आगमाः प्रमाणानि। (आगम=आप्त वचन)-समाधिपाद-7

(Perception, inference, and testimony are the sources of knowledge.)

Perception by senses is the main source of knowledge. However, sometimes perception may be erroneous or illusory due to some defects. The causes of illusion have been classified as: 1. defects in sense-organs, 2. presentation of part or an aspect instead of the whole object, and 3. mental prejudice.

Anuman or inference is the knowledge derived from another knowledge. It includes both deduction and induction. Comparison is the means by which we gain knowledge of a thing from its similarity to another thing previously well-known. The above sources of knowledge are also true for science.

In science, every truth must be logical, but in philosophy, which is a part of *Dharma*, there are many subjects of metaphysics that cannot come under the scope of reasoning. They transcend empirical and logical knowledge. A famous western philosopher, *Immanuel Kant* of the nineteenth century, is also of the view that the moral basis of religion should not be derived from reason alone; it must be derived from the inner self by direct perception or intuitive insight.

One of the chief sources of this knowledge is testimony or knowledge received from authority. We can learn a good deal from standard testimony (*Shabda*) or scriptural revelations or an able Guru. Upanishad means 'to sit near (*Guru*)'. An able *Guru* is the main source, especially for transcendental knowledge.

Upanishads are mainly received by disciples from *Gurus* in a question-answer form. In Gitā 4.34, *Lord Krishna* advises to receive knowledge from an able *Guru* in a humble way. But in this situation, who is the right person whose words are worthy to be believed?

The Upanishad warns :

अंधेनैव नीयमाना यथान्धाः ..। कठोपनिषद् 1.2.5 मुण्डकोपनिषद 1.2.8

(A blind must not lead a blind)

Again Kathopanishad says :

अनन्यप्रोक्ते गतिः अत्र न अस्ति अणीयान् हि अतर्क्यम् अणुप्रमाणात्।1.2.8 (*Ătmatatva*, matters related to Soul or metaphysics, are subtler than the subtlest and these could not be understood without the sermon or the help of the right person or *Guru* because these are beyond the limit of logic or reasoning.)

In the *Kathopanishad*, *Yama* suggests *Nachiketa*:

प्रेष्ठ(प्रिय! (नचिकेता) न एषा मतिः तर्केण न आपनेया...'

(This knowledge (about the soul or *Brahmăjnăn*) cannot be achieved by reasoning or logic.)

Then, who can have this knowledge?

Mudakonishad explains -

'न चक्षुषा गृहते नापि वाचा न अन्य देवैः तपसा कर्मणा वा।
ज्ञान प्रसादेन विशुद्ध सत्त्व तु तम् पश्यते निष्कलं(अवयवरहित)ध्यायमानः।'
मुण्डकोपनिषद 3.1.8

(That who has no body parts (dimensionless) cannot be perceived by eyes, cannot be described by words, cannot be known by penance of gods or their endeavors, that can be realised by enlightenment of the *purged* soul by meditation.)

Again the *Upanishad* says:

भिद्यते (खुल जाती है) हृदयग्रन्थिः अस्य छिद्यन्ते सर्व संशयः।
क्षीयन्ते तस्य कर्माणि तस्मिन् दृष्टे परापरे । 2.2.8

(Whose fetters or complexes of the heart are terminated, and all doubts removed, the effects of his deeds on the pure soul are cleared, that very person can have the realization of both worldly and transcendental.)

Rishis have these qualities, who had tried to know about all the subtle matters by their penance, and exercise their insight for thousands of years, and the knowledge has been saved in scriptures like *Vedas*, *Upanishads*.

'Brahmasutra' opines:

श्रुतत्वाच्च । ब्रह्मसूत्र 1.1.11

(And (*Brahma*) can be known with the help of *Shruti* (*Vedas*, *Upanishads*.))

So, as regards transcendental knowledge, testimony is the source of knowledge. In *Sanătan Dharma*, *Vedas*, *Upanishads*, *Brahmasutra*, and *Bhagavat Gită* are commonly accepted by all as authentic Scriptures.

Some thinkers like *Maharshi Kapil*, the founder of the *Sănkhya* System, or *Buddha* ruled out the need for discussing these matters and took no interest in even speaking a word about the matters that are beyond the conception of the human mind. They thought that the Creator of the universe is not required to explain nature and human behaviour. So, they ignored God. The entire universe (प्रकृति) is governed by well-defined cosmic laws (ऋत). They are of the view that *Prakriti*, space, and time (*Dik*, *Kăl*) are without beginning and end. They are ever-existing. Even in the *Gită*, one can find a similarity with this view when *Lord Krishna* says: 'Never was there a time when I did not exist, nor you, nor all these kings; nor in the future shall any of us cease to be.' *Gită 2.12* So, they laid emphasis on the functions and methods related to the purification, the elevation of the soul resulting in the welfare and upliftment of self and all; to get rid of the cycle of birth and death, the cause of suffering. This should be the ultimate goal of any being. *Maharshi Kapil*, the founder of the *Sănkhya System*, is the seer of great importance. Maximum principles of the world-famous *Yoga* System, the work of *Maharshi Patanjali*, and *Buddhism* were greatly influenced by *Sănkhya Darshan*. *Yoga Darshan* is also called *Seshwar Sănkhya*, which means *'Sănkhya* with God.' Patanjali advocated adoration of God, perhaps because Patanjali thought that in spite of all efforts, Divine Grace matters. Faith and reverence (श्रद्धा) to Almighty are great positive thoughts that are important factors for spiritual growth

तीव्रसंवेगानाम् आसनः। समाधिपाद- 21(पातंजलयोगप्रदीप)
ईश्वरप्रणिधानात् वा । समाधिपाद- 23
स्मृतिपरिशुद्धौ .....।। समाधिपाद-43

(By deeper emotions, the success (in *Samădhi*) comes nearer. And also by God-meditation. And by purification of the Soul.)

CHAPTER : 6

BROAD MINDED AND UNIVERSAL APPROACH

Just like scientists, *Rishis* never opine that their statements are final. They are always ready to welcome new ideas and thoughts that seem to be superior or more beneficial.

The *Rigveda* is the oldest literature in the world, which desires:

आ नो भद्राः क्रतवो यन्तु विश्वतो अदब्धासो अपरितास उद्भिदः।
देवा नो यथासदमिद् वृधे असन्नाप्रायुवो रक्षितोरो दिवे दिवे।
ऋग्वेद1.89.1 देवता- विश्वदेवाः

("Let the noble, sublime thoughts of the world come from all directions, taking us to higher levels. Let the gods, who protect us, increase our progress.")

Sanătan Dharma is not a closed religion. It remains open to sublime changes and is as clean as a flowing stream. Being so old, the appearance of some flaws cannot be ruled out, but Hindus are not unwilling to listen to them and make amendments. Ultimately, free choice is the evergreen solution. In Hinduism, faith and search go hand in hand. Where there are closed faiths, there are possibilities of quarrels. This is not the case with Hindus. Most Hindus do various practices, pray to gods, worship deities, chant *mantras*, meditate on Om or the symbol of the formless God. They respect all *Sanătan* faiths. In the olden days, there were some natural differences for superiority, but Hinduism has always been open to amendments. It is not a locked religion.

In the *Kathopanishad*, the *Rishi* gives latitude to toil hard to attain knowledge of the best and the excellent.

उत्तिष्ठत जाग्रत प्राप्य वरान्निबोधत।
क्षुरस्य धारा निशिता(तीक्ष्ण की हुई)दुरत्यया दुर्गम् कवयः वदन्ति ।
कठोपनिषद 1.3.14

("Wake up, rise, and attain knowledge of the best and excellent. (But it is not easy) The learned people say that it is a difficult task, like walking on the sharp edge of a sword.")

The *Mundakopanishad* and *Kathopanishad* also warn to be careful about choosing the Guru. During *Buddha's* time, there were numerous sects and *Gurus*, making it a confusing situation. Therefore, he advises not to follow any Guru blindly but to enlighten oneself.

Mahătma Buddha advised:

अप्प दीपो भव।

("Be your own light.")

Jains also have a similar view:

णो लोगस्स एसणं चरे- (किसीका अनुसरण मत करो)। पुरिसा!
तुमेव तुम मित्तं। भगवान महावीर

("Don't follow anybody; you are the friend of yourself.")

Rishis pray for the welfare of all living and non-living beings, not just a section of mankind. In the *Vedas*, it has been wished many times:

'तन्मे मनः शिवसंकल्पमस्तु।

("May my mind wish for the welfare of all.")

'सर्वभूतेषु चात्मानं ततो न विजुगुप्सते।' मंत्र 6 ईशावास्योपनिषद

("View every being as yourself; do not hate.")

In *Gitǎ*, Shree Krishna says that:

'ते प्राप्नुवन्ति मामेव सर्व भूतहितेरताः। गीता 12.4

("The person engaged in the welfare of all living beings ultimately achieves Me.")

'सुहृदं सर्वभूतानां ज्ञात्वा मां शान्तिमृच्छति। गीता 5.29.

("The benefactor and well-wisher of all living entities attains peace.")

'निर्वैरः सर्वभूतेषु यः स मामेति पाण्डव। गीता 11.55

("*O Arjuna*! The one who is friendly to every living being will certainly come to Me.")

Upanishads are full of similar Slokas. Our *Rishis* are filled with love for all living beings and non-living entities as well. *Sanătan Dharma* never talks about any sect or section of people; it is a universal religion that preaches for the welfare of not only human beings but also all living and non-living beings of creation.

In different religious scriptures of *Sanătan Dharma*, views may slightly differ because they are the opinions of different Rishis, but their goal is similar. The *Dharma*, especially the great *Shrimad Bhagvad Gită* which we call *Gită*, tries to coordinate or harmonize different sects of *Sanătan Dharma* and other religions with statements like:

ये यथा मां प्रपद्यन्ते तांस्तथैव भजाम्यहम्।
मम वर्त्माः (पथ) अनुवर्तन्ते मनुष्याः पार्थ सर्वशः। गीता 4.11

("By whatever way one seeks me, I accept them the same way. O son of *Pritha*! Everyone follows my path in all respects.")

यो यो यां यां तनुं भक्तः श्रद्धा अर्चितुम् इच्छति।
तस्य तस्य अचलां श्रद्धां ताम् एव विदधामि अहम्। गीता 7/21

(When one desires to worship a particular deity, surely, I make their faith steady (so that they can devote themselves to the particular deity with faith.)")

Gită also seeks to establish harmony among different sects of Hinduism when Krishna says: 'I am *Ram* among the warriors' and 'I am *Shiva* among *Rudras*.'

Some thinkers opine that *Maharshi Kapil*, the founder of the *Sănkhya* School of Indian Philosophy, is an atheist because there is no place for God in his famous philosophy of *Sănkhya*. To remove this disrespect; in *Gită*, *Krishna* says: 'I am Kapil *Muni* among enlightened ones.'

The Gită is one of the most popular scriptures in the world. It has been translated into more than 500 languages. It has been truly said: 'Gită is the most beautiful, perhaps the only true philosophical song existing in any known tongue.'

- William von Humboldt

Sanătan Dharma always prays for the welfare of all and strives to foster harmony among the religions of the world. The invaders like Greeks, Persians, Mongols, and Huns who came to India willingly embraced *Sanătan Dharma*, but Hindus never compelled them to do so.

CHAPTER : 7

CAUSE AND EFFECT THEORY AND THE THEORY OF EVOLUTION

The cause-effect theory forms the basis and backbone of science, stating that every effect must have a cause. No change is non-causal in this ever-changing world. Spirituality is also a science that falls under the scope of the cause-effect theory.

This theory is one of the central features of the *Sănkhya* philosophy, known as *Satkăryavăd* (सत्कार्यवाद). *Buddhism* also supports the cause and effect theory, known as *Pratityasamutpăd* (प्रतीत्यसमुत्पाद). *Maharshi Kanăda*, the founder of the *Vaisheshik* school, has also supported this theory. According to this theory, every effect has some cause, and the effect exists beforehand in its cause. There is no such thing as total destruction.

As a result, *Sănkhya* also adopts the theory of involution and evolution. The world has phenomenal reality, constantly undergoing transformation. The cycle of evolution and reabsorption has never had a beginning. Every phenomenon of cosmic evolution is characterized by activity and change. All things go through infinitesimal changes of growth and decay. In the smallest instant of time (*Kshan*), the whole universe undergoes a change. In this sense, the universe is neither real nor unreal. This theory of *Sănkhya Darshan* is analogous to modern science.

According to *Vishishtădvaita* (qualified monism or qualified non-dualism) of *Rămanujăchărya*, there is an interesting and logical explanation of evolution. The theory states that *Brahma* with attributes or *Lord Nărayan* exists in nature as Existence (*Sat*), Consciousness (*Chit*), and Bliss (*Ănand*). The universe is the manifested form of the Lord, and it also possesses all three attributes but in different stages. In inanimate matter, there is Sat, but Chit and *Ănand* are in dormant states. When suitable conditions appear, the *Chit* starts to awaken, and the inanimate becomes animate. As the amount of *Chit* (Consciousness) increases, *Ănand* increases, and evolution starts. *Ănand* (bliss) is proportional to *Chit* (Consciousness). When the Chit increases, it is called evolution. As the Chit increases, the willpower to live and prosper increases, and thus evolution takes place. At the human stage, consciousness is abundant. Finally, at this stage, by enhancing consciousness (*Chit*) through righteousness, a purified soul, and the grace of God, a stage is reached when *Chit* and *Ănand* are fully awakened, and the soul becomes *Sacchidănand* (*Sat Chit Ananda*) and attains salvation.

In Bhakti, the soul does not merge into *Brahma* but enjoys a *separate* personal existence and lives with *Brahma* (*Lord Nărayan*) in *Vaikunth* and enjoys eternal bliss.

According to *Shrimad Bhăgavata Pură na*, there are ten *Avatărs* (manifestations) of *Vishnu*. The first one is *Matsya* (fish), which entirely lives in water. The second *Avatăr* is

Kurma (turtle), which can live in water and on land. The third one is *Varăha* (boar), a four-footed animal of the land. Next is *Narasimha* (man-lion), half man and half animal, followed by *Vămana* (dwarf). Then comes the stage of incarnations of *Vishnu* in the form of complete men like *Parăshurăma, Răma, Shri Krishna, Buddha,* and lastly *Kalki*, who is to come at the end of *Kăliyuga*.

The above statements of the *Purăna* indicate the evolution of species on Earth and seem to be in agreement with Darwin's Theory. Hindu scriptures like the *Vishistădvaita* theory or the *Prakriti-Purusha* theory of *Sănkhya Darshan* agree with the latest theory of evolution. They never advocate an irrational idea that life on Earth began with man.

CHAPTER : 8
LAW OF KARMA

Famous Law of *Karma* of Hindus is also similar to the theory of cause and effect. It has already been mentioned about *Rit* (Cosmic Law). The universe is governed by this law, which pervades the entire cosmos. This concept holds great significance, and the Law of *Karma* is derived from the *Rit*.

According to the theory of *Karma*, whatever actions we perform, whether good or bad, by mind, word, or body, the corresponding results (effects) automatically manifest sooner or later. As the famous scientist Einstein said, "God does not play dice with the universe," indicating that nothing is random in the universe.

Rit can be likened to the algorithm of a computer for the Cosmos. We input our deeds, and the results are automatic. Whether our deeds are good or bad, they come around sooner or later. The designer of this invisible algorithm is referred to as Cosmic Consciousness.

In reality, all deeds, whether good or bad, leave imprints on the subtle body or personal soul due to *Ahankăr*, the ego of doership. These imprints are the cause of bondage, pleasure, or pain, and they also contribute to the creation of one's nature. They are also the cause of rebirth, a concept Hindus have faith in, and which is now considered to be an almost proven fact. After death, the physical body is destroyed, but the subtle body (सूक्ष्म शरीर) along with the personal soul (जीवात्मा) continues to exist.

We can find the references of rebirth in *Upanishads* and Gită.

प्राप्य पुण्यकृतां लोकान् उषित्वा शाश्वतीः समाः।
शुचीनां श्रीमतां गेहे योगभ्रष्टः अभिजायते । गीता 6.41

(The unsuccessful *Yogi*, after many years of enjoyment on the planets of the pious living entities due to their righteous deeds, is born into a family of righteous people.)

It is essential to point out that in this *Sloka*, *Lord Krishna* mentions a planet in this universe better than Earth with more pleasure and comfort, which we may call heaven, attained after life as a result of good deeds in one's lifetime.

To achieve enlightenment or salvation, one must rid themselves of the stored imprints that act as fetters. True happiness ultimately arises from a spiritual quest and the enhancement of consciousness. We must expand our heart and mind until we break the chains of ego. Giving up the pride of doership does not mean inaction, but one should not be attached to or lustful towards the result of their actions.

As stated in the *Gită*:

कर्मण्येवाधिकारस्ते मा फलेषु कदाचन । गीता 2.47

(You have a right to perform your prescribed duties, but you are not entitled to the fruits of your actions.)

Deeds are not only physical; they can also be mental, verbal, or spiritual. *Rishis* advise us to act mindfully and righteously in the present moment, as our future depends on our present deeds.

आत्मैव हि आत्मनो बन्धन्धुः आत्मा एव रिपुः आत्मनः। गीता 6.5

(One is one's own friend and foe as well.)

According to the recent developments in medical science, the mental waves of a dying person have been studied, revealing that all the impressions of life's deeds move rapidly, like a reel, during 30 seconds before and 30 seconds after the heart's closure. This situation also contributes to bondage and rebirth, a realization that seems to have been known to the *Rishis*.

So, in the *Gită*, *Lord Krishna* advises the solution:

बुद्धियुक्तो जहाति इह उभे सुकृत दुष्कृते ।
तस्मात् योगाय युज्यस्व योगः कर्मसु कौशलम्। गीता 2/50

('A person who is learned rids himself of both good and bad deeds in this life. Therefore, strive for Yoga, which is the art of all work.)

Again, he says:

मयि सर्वाणि कर्माणि संन्यस्य अध्यात्म चेतसा ।
निराशीः निर्ममः भूत्वा युध्यस्व विगतज्वरः। गीता 3/30

(Therefore, surrendering all your works unto Me, with full knowledge of Me, without any desire for gain, and free from the ego of the doer, and without being lethargic, fight (perform))

Again, *Lord Krishna* specifically says:

ओम् इति एकाक्षरम् ब्रह्म व्याहरन् मम् अनुस्मरन् ।
यः प्रयाति त्यजन् देहम् सः याति परमाम् गतिम् । गीता 8.13

(If one vibrates *Om*, the symbol of *Brahma*, and thinks of Me at the time of leaving the body, he attains the ultimate destination.)

In addition to the Theory of *Karma*, in *Purănas*, the theory of hell and heaven is also adopted in Hinduism, but as I think, it is meant for the common people who have no time or mental depth to think logically. According to this theory, the result of bad deeds is painful hell, and that of good deeds is pleasant heaven. Although heaven has been mentioned in the *Gită* as a result of good deeds, it is a source of temporary pleasure, which is inferior to the benevolent path of permanent bliss and the consciousness of Eternity achieved through *Yoga*.

In the Gită (6.41), 'a planet of pious living entities' (पुण्यकृतां लोकान्) has been mentioned as heaven.

Buddhism and *Jainism* also support the Cause-Effect theory and the theory of *Karma*.

Some atheists like *Chărvak Muni* have no faith in the theory of *Karma*. He said:

यावत जीवेत, सुखम् जीवेत, ऋणम् कृत्वा घृतम् पीवेत।
भस्मिभूतस्य शरीरस्य पुनर्जन्मो कुतः।

(As long as you live, live happily, even by taking a loan. How will the dead body, which has been burnt, take rebirth?)

CHAPTER 9
THEORY OF REINCARNATION

Hindus believe in the theory of reincarnation or rebirth. After death, the physical body is gone, but the consciousness or the personal soul (जीवात्मा) which is imperishable continues its journey by taking rebirth with a suitable body.

वासांसि जीर्णानि यथा विहाय नवानि गृह्णाति नरोऽपराणि ।
तथा शरीराणि विहाय जीर्णा- न्यन्यानि संयाति नवानि देही ॥ गीता 2.22

(As a person puts on new garments, giving up old one, similarly, the soul accepts new material bodies, giving up the old and useless ones.)

This theory is also related to the theory of *Karma*, where the new body depends mostly on the deeds of the previous life. Every deed in life leaves an impression on the personal soul of the individual due to the ego of doership. These imprints are the cause of bondage, which creates the nature of the personal soul, and it is automatically attracted to a new body of the same nature and environment during rebirth. Jainism also supports the view that the personal soul is attracted towards the *Pudgal* (physical body) of the same nature, while *Buddhism* also approves the theory of rebirth.

Ultimately, *Sanătan Dharma* is of the view that the result of good deeds is pleasure, and that of bad deeds is suffering in this life or future life. To mitigate and remove these impressions, the cause of bondage and rebirth, one needs to address the ego of doership, which is the main culprit.

In the *Gită*, *Lord Krishna* says:

कामक्रोध विमुक्तानां यतीनां यतचेतसाम् ।
अभितो ब्रह्मनिर्वाणं वर्तते विदितात्मनाम् । गीता 5.26

(The sage who is free from desires and irritation, who has control over thoughts and knowledge of the spiritual world, will attain liberation in the near future.)

Lord Krishna advises surrendering the result of all deeds to God. In *Gită chapter-5*, this matter has been described in detail. The theory of reincarnation is a widely accepted concept supported by numerous observations, thousands of examples, and research conducted by several doctors in Western universities.

CHAPTER 10

ATOMIC THEORY AND NEWTON'S LAWS

In modern science, John Dalton is credited for proposing the atomic theory in 1810 CE. The basic theory states that each element is made up of fundamental units called atoms, which are the fundamental units of matter.

Maharshi Kanăd, the founder of *Vaisheshika* School of Indian philosophy, proposed the atomic theory of the universe. *Kanăd* was a *Rishi* of antiquity, even before *Buddha*. The word *'Kanăd'* originates from the basic root of *'Kana,'* which means particle.

Vaisheshika is one of the six systems of Indian philosophy, and its name originates from the *Sanskrit* root *'Vishesha,'* which stands for atomic individuality. It seems that the *Sanskrit* word *'Anu'* has been translated as *'atom.'*

According to the atomic theory of *Kanăd*, the universe has been formed by the aggregation of atoms, which are eternal.

परमाणु नित्यम् परिमण्डलम् ।

(Atom is eternal and spherical.)

An atom has been defined as something existing, eternal, and having no cause. It is less than the least, invisible, indivisible, intangible, and imperceptible by the senses. Atoms are of different kinds, each possessing its own distinct individuality (*Vishesha*), which is the root and cause of the name of the school *Vaisheshika*. *Maharshi Kanăda* explained that atoms are naturally passive, and their movement is due to some external impact. This statement shows quite good congruence with Newton's First Law of Motion, which states that *'the body at rest will remain at rest unless acted upon by some force.'*

Kanăda lived in prehistoric times, before *Buddha* and even before *Rishi Gautam*, the founder of the *Nyăya* School of Indian philosophy. *Nyăya* and *Vaisheshika* are different schools, but both are analytical types of philosophies, based on logic and reasoning, and they agree on their basic principles. *Jainism* is also a logical and analytical philosophy with a similar atomic theory. According to this philosophy, matter is called Pudgala, which means *'that which is liable to integrate and disintegrate.'* The smallest part of matter that cannot be further divided, being partless, is called Parmănus or atoms. The physical objects apprehended by the senses consist of atoms. A homogeneous mass object (*Pudgal*) breaks up into several kinds of atoms by differentiation. An atom has no beginning and end. It is not perceivable (*Amurta*), although it is the basis of all perceivable objects (*Murta*). An atom has weight. Material things are produced by the combination of atoms, which are subject to mutual attraction. The attraction of atoms has been admitted.

The above statement reminds us of Newton's law of universal gravitation, published in 1687 CE, which states that *'each particle attracts every other particle in the universe.'*

CHAPTER 11

LAW OF CONSERVATION OF MATTER AND ENERGY

The law of conservation of matter and energy states: *'matter and energy are neither created nor destroyed but only changed from one form to another.'* The law was discovered by Antoine Lavoisier in 1785 CE, and it states that 'matter is neither created nor destroyed.' Then, in 1842 CE, Julius Robert Mayer discovered the law of conservation of energy. Einstein later revealed that mass and energy are different forms of the same thing and they may be interchanged. Humans do not have the ability to create or destroy energy or matter. At present, this theory is being used in many fields of science.

According to *Sănkhya Darshan*, every effect has a cause, meaning the effect is the manifested condition of some cause. This is not new creation; it is also associated with the law of conservation.

In the *Gită*, it is said:

ना असतो विद्यते भावो न अभावो विद्यते सतः ।
उभयोरपि दृष्टः अन्तः तु अनयो तत्त्वदर्शिभिः । गीता 2.16

(Those who are the seers of truth have concluded both the facts that which exists never ceases to exist and that which has no existence will never exist.)

Again, in *Sănkhya Darshan*, *Maharshi Kapila* says:

ना वस्तुनो वस्तु सिद्धिः ।

(Nothing cannot be the cause of something.)

According to the theory of *Satkăryavăd* of *Sănkhya Darshan*, the effect produced already exists in the cause in the potential condition. A thing is always produced, never created. Production is a manifested condition. So, there is no new creation or destruction but only transformation, manifestation, and non-manifestation.

As stated earlier, in accordance with *Vaisheshik* and *Jain* philosophies, all the physical objects of the universe are made up of atoms, which are eternal. The above philosophical statements of *Sanătan Dharma* have predicted the modern theory of conservation of matter and energy long ago.

CHAPTER 12
THEORY OF RELATIVITY

According to the basic theory of relativity, any statement or judgment about any object is not absolute but relative to the viewpoint or frame of reference of the viewer.

The *Shyădvăd* (स्याद्वाद) Theory of Jainism is similar to the theory of relativity, stating that every statement or judgment we pass in our daily life about any object is true only in reference to the standpoint and aspect of the object concerned. *Shyăd* means *'in some respect'*. When viewed differently, we often disagree and quarrel, even in philosophical discussions.

This observer-based judgment is also called *Andh-Gaja-Naya* (अंध-गज-नय) in Hindu scriptures, which means the different views of the blind about the shape of an elephant. The different views may be partially true, just like the different descriptions of the blind men. Each blind man had a different view based on the part of the elephant they touched. The quarrel was resolved as soon as they realised that their knowledge was only partial.

There are three dimensions of space to define the position of an object. Later on, the fourth dimension, time, was introduced by scientists. According to modern science, both time and space are related, but none of them is absolute; they are variables. In *Sanătan Dharma*, space and time (दिक् काल) both were given importance from the very beginning. During the creation of the universe, time and space were the first creations. Modern science agrees with this view.

The above ideas of Jainism and *Upanishads* are in agreement with the theory of relativity.

CHAPTER 13
QUANTUM THEORY AND UNITY IN DIVERSITY

"After the conversation about Indian philosophy, some of the Quantum Physicists that had seemed crazy suddenly made much more sense."

-W. Heisenberg, a German Physicist

"If you want to find the secret of the universe, think in terms of energy, frequency, and vibration."

-Nikola Tesla, American physicist

Science and Indian philosophy both find unity in diversity. Several forces are active in the universe - gravitational force, electromagnetic force, nuclear force. Science is trying to explain the origin and concept of these forces. Many theories are proposed by scientists - *General Theory of Relativity, Quantum Theory, String Theory, etc.*

Quantum theory was proposed by *Niels Bohr* and *Max Planck* won the *Nobel Prize for Physics in 1921.* The Nobel Prize of Physics in 2022 is also related to quantum physics. This theory is the theoretical basis of modern physics that explains the nature and behaviour of matter and energy, according to which matter and energy are waves or vibrations at the subatomic level. There is no rigidity at this level, and there are only fuzzy waves. Different particles in the universe are due to the difference in the wave frequencies or wave functions. So, the core of every element is nothing but vibrations.

Quantum theory intends to state that truth has two levels - at a gross level, all objects exist as particles, whereas at a subtle level, they exist as waves or energy. Like Quantum science, *Upanishads* also advocate the duality of reality. They categorize the entire knowledge in two forms - परा, अपरा means transcendental and non-transcendental, that is subtle and gross. Living beings exist in a gross form as physical bodies and also as subtle bodies. Similarly, God has two forms - Creation and Creator as formless *Brahma*.

It has already been mentioned while discussing the creation of the universe that the *Rigveda*, the oldest literature of the world, affirms -

प्राण एजति निःसृतम्।

(The creation has been ejected by the vibration of Consciousness).

The entire creation, including truth and fallacy, has evolved from the vibration of the Cosmic Consciousness, and every particle of the universe is interconnected. There are vibrations, Divinity, and harmony at the core of every particle. It has also been mentioned in *Upanishads* that when *Brahma* wished to be many (to create the universe), He energized Himself. So, at the core of the universe, there are two things - energy and consciousness.

The *Sunyavăd* (शून्य वाद) of *Nagărjuna* (C150 - C 250), a *Buddhist* saint, is also of similar view. His *Sunya* does not mean exactly the vacuum or nothingness, but he wants to state that our dictionary of words has been developed by the sensory world, although the reality is beyond that, which our words would fail to capture.

Adishankarăchărya, a saint of the 8th century, who expounded the theory of Advait or non-dualism, suggests that there is underlying oneness to all existence. There is one substratum of reality, the *Brahma*. The sensory world is *Măyă*, which refers to the illusory nature of the world.

According to *Adi Shankar*, the highest form of reality is non-duality.

He tells -

ब्रह्म सत्यम् जगन्मिथ्या।

(*Brahma* or Cosmic Consciousness is only true, the world is illusory.)

Shankar does not deny the perceptual world, but he is of the view that what we perceive by senses is not the absolute truth. The *Măyă* or illusion exists till wisdom dawns in. *Shankar* gives the example of a piece of rope lying in darkness. We can perceive it as a snake until sufficient light appears. As the quantum theory describes two realities at the subatomic and atomic level, similarly *Shankarăchărya* described two levels of realities, absolute reality (*Parmarthik Satya*) and practical reality (*Vyăvahărik* Satys).

Brahma is the absolute reality while *Măyă* (the physical world) is not absolute reality, it is relative reality and apparent reality.

Sanătan Philosophy has a simple solution for the amazing and puzzling recent discovery regarding Quantum Physics.

In *Gită Lord Krishna* says:

अविभक्तं च भूतेषु विभक्तमिव च स्थितम्। गीता 13.16

(Although the supersoul appears to be divided among all beings, He is undivided.)

Scriptures say:

'न इह नानास्ति किंचन।' कठोपनिषद 2/1/11

(There is nothing like duality here.)

Shivasutra says: (3.3)

('Illusion is caused by ignorance, the inability to discern the nature of elements.')

The modern scientist of the USA, Kelvin Lesko, says - *"What is this great place I live in? Right now, 95 per cent of it is a mystery."*

We are in illusion and darkness. So, the *Rishi* desires -

तमसो मा ज्योतिर्गमय।

(Let us move from darkness (ignorance) to light (wisdom))

At the core, all beings are interconnected. Vibration and Consciousness are the core of all beings.

In *Gitǎ Lord Krishna* says:

भूतानाम् अस्मि चेतना।

(I (*Brahma*) am present in all beings as consciousness.)

So, the *Upanishads* state:

अहम् ब्रह्मास्मि। तत् त्वम् असि।

(I am *Brahma*, and the same you are.)

Will *Durant*, a famous American writer, found similarity between Quantum theory and *Vedic* philosophy. In his book *'Great Minds and Ideas of All Time,'* he writes:

"In fact, many early quantum researchers such as Schrodinger, Heisenberg, and Bohr have been exposed to Vedic philosophy."

He intends to tell that these scientists were inspired by the great *Vedic* philosophy.

CHAPTER 14
CREATION OF THE UNIVERSE

About the creation of the universe, the *Rigveda* states:

यदिदं किंचित् जगत् सर्वं प्राण एजति निःसृतम्। ऋग्वेद 3.12.7

(The entire universe has been ejected from the vibration of Consciousness.)

Modern science has also arrived at the conclusion that all matter and energy ultimately resolve into a state of pure vibration at the subtle level. Research in quantum physics is now finding that there is no rigidity at the subatomic level. Matter consists of fuzzy waves that can manifest as particles.

According to the cause and effect theory, there must be some cause behind the creation. Naturally, the cause should be the Supreme Energy, which is the cause of all causes. (कारणं कारणानाम्।) The creation is ejected by the vibration of Consciousness.

According to modern science, the universe appeared from singularity. Before the creation of the universe, there was nothingness, as mentioned in the *Taittiriyopanishad*. The scripture also opines that during the creation of the universe, the first thing that appeared was an egg-shaped dazzling golden embryo (हिरण्यमाण्ड, हिरण्यगर्भ) as a seed, containing time and space. From that seed, matter, energy (रयि), and consciousness (प्राण) were ejected with light and sound.

सः अकामयत। बहु स्यां प्रजायेय इति। सः तपः अतप्यत।
इदम् सर्वम् असृजत। तैत्तिरीय उपनिषद्, बल्ली 2

(He (*Brahma*) desired, *"Let there be many."* He invoked His will-power and got energized. By the energy, the entire universe has been created.)

It would be interesting to understand and acknowledge what elements appeared first at the time of creation and how far they are congruent with modern science. According to the *Upanishads*, the creation has been ejected from an infinite Conscious Energy. The universe has been so harmoniously, scientifically, judiciously planned, and intellectually designed that nobody can deny the presence of an infinite Conscious Power behind it. The great scientist Einstein also shared the view that the universe is not a random creation.

Matter and anti-matter

According to the *Upanishads*, *Brahma* has created the universe and entered it, becoming both truth and fallacy, knowledge and confusion, describable and indescribable. This means He became all opposites.

इदम् सर्वम् असृजत। तत् सृष्ट्वा तत् एव अनुप्रविशत्। तत् अनुप्रविश्य सत् च असत् च अभवत्। निरुक्तं च अनिरुक्तं च। विज्ञानं च अविज्ञानं च। सत्यं च अनृतं च सत्यम् अभवत्। यत इदं किं च। तैत्तिरीय उपनिषद 2.6

(He created all. After creating, He entered into that, He became truth and fallacy, describable and indescribable, conscious and unconscious, and whatsoever.)

In the *Bhagvad Gitǎ*, *Lord Krishna* says:

सत् असत् च अहम् अर्जुन। गीता 9/19

(*O Arjuna*! I am both truth and fallacy.)

In the spiritual world, *Vidyǎ* (truth) and *Avidyǎ* (fallacy) are opposing forces. They are like centripetal and centrifugal forces that balance each other. *Vidyǎ* is a centripetal force that helps the soul move towards the Super Centre, while *Avidyǎ* is a force of destruction that tries to disturb this movement and keeps the soul away from the Super Soul.

विद्या अविद्ये निहिते यत्र गूढे।

(Here, truth and fallacy both reside in a hidden state.)

Lord Buddha named this *Avidyǎ* as *Mǎr*, which disturbed him during the process of enlightenment. *Upanishads* pray to God:

तमसो मा ज्योतिर्गमय।

(Let us move from darkness to light.)

Even an able *Guru* may be a helper.

Gu stands for darkness, and *Ru* stands for light.

A *Guru* is the person who leads from darkness to light.

Truth and fallacy balance each other, and balance is the secret of existence.

Upanishads are optimistic and say:

सत्यमेव जयति नानृतम्। बृहदारण्यक उपनिषद

(Ultimately, truth will emerge victorious, not fallacy.)

Sănkhya Darshan, one of the six schools of Indian philosophy, opines that Prakriti is the fundamental substance out of which the universe evolves. In its fundamental condition, *Prakriti* is a mix of all pairs of opposites.

In the material world, every elementary particle has a corresponding antiparticle, which is antimatter. Neutrons have anti-neutrons, electrons have anti-electrons, which are also called positrons. According to modern science, the universe is expanding at an accelerated rate, and for this, a force opposite to the force of gravity is conceived. Not knowing what this energy could be, it is named dark energy, or there may be an anti-universe beyond, which exerts the force of attraction for its expansion with acceleration.

Time and space

The *Upanishad* states -

तस्मात् वै एतस्मात् आत्मनः आकाशः सम्भूतः।
तैत्तिरीय उपनिषद्, बल्ली 2.1

(Surely, from Consciousness, space was produced.)

According to the *Vaisheshik* School of Indian philosophy, founded by *Maharshi Kanăda,* time (काल) is one of the causative elements (कारण द्रव्य) for the creation of the universe. Additionally, according to the *Shvetăshvatar Upanishad* (1.1.2), time is one of the fundamental elements of creation.

Big Bang Theory

The Big Bang Theory is a widely accepted explanation for the origin and evolution of the universe. According to this theory, the universe was nonexistent before, then it rapidly expanded from a highly dense singularity through a massive explosion, gradually reaching its current size, and continues to expand.

Now, the *Upanishads* state:

असत् वाइदमग्र आसीत। तो वै सदजायत्। (तैत्तिरीयोपनिषद्).

(In the beginning, it was non-existent, from which existence emerged.)

As stated by the *Upanishads*, the universe emerged from a seed called *Hiranyagarbha* or *Hiranyamănd*, which signifies an 'egg-shaped golden embryo.'

According to the *Prashnopanishad* (1.4, 1.5), during the creation of the universe, matter, energy (रयि), and consciousness emerged, accompanied by a profound light and sound.

Describing the generated light, the *Rishi* articulates:

'thousands of sun-rays converged - That One - I perceived the glorious form of God.' Rigved 5.62.1.

The *Bhagvad Gită* states -

दिवि सूर्यसहस्रस्य भवेत् युगपत् उत्थिता।
यदि भाः सदृशी सा स्यात् भासः तस्य महात्मनः। 11/12

(If a thousand suns were to rise simultaneously in the sky, their radiance might resemble the effulgence of the Supreme Person in that universal form.)

The sound generated during the Big Bang resembled the Om sound. This is why Om is referred to as *Pranava*, denoting the primal sound of the universe. These assertions align with the concepts of the Big Bang Theory.

According to the cause and effect theory, there must be a cause for the big bang. What triggered the Big Bang or creation? The *Upanishads* address this in their unique manner.

The *Rishi* states:

जन्माद्यस्य यतः। ब्रह्मसूत्र 1.1.2

(*Brahma* is the cause of creation.)

What is the evidence?

Brahmasutra provides an answer:

अत एव प्राणः। ब्रह्मसूत्र 1.1.23

(Consciousness exists in the universe due to Him.)

तत् तु समन्वयात्। ब्रह्मसूत्र 1.1.4

(Harmony and coordination exist in the universe due to Him.)

Steady State Theory about the creation of universe

As an alternative to the Big Bang Theory, some scientists of the 20th century developed a theory of the creation of the universe called the 'steady-state theory.' This theory states that the universe is infinite in extent, infinitely old, and it exists at all times in the past and will exist at all times in the future.

When dealing with matters that are not easily conceived, scientists propose different theories. Similarly, the *Rishis* have also presented various theories, but their primary objective is not worldly exploration but spiritual development. Like the steady-state theory, *Sănkhya Darshan* also states that *Prakriti* is *Anădi* (the universe is without a beginning), and there is no need for an intelligent creator. *Jainism* also holds the view that the atoms (*Anu*), which constitute the world, have no specific point of beginning or end.

CHAPTER 15

MATHEMATICS AND ASTRONOMY

"We owe a lot to the Indians, who taught us how to count, without which no worthwhile scientific discovery could have been made."

-Albert Einstein

"There has been no more revolutionary contribution than the one which the Hindus made when they invented zero."

-Lancelot Hogben, English Mathematician

It is fascinating to know that Mathematics (*Ganit*) is also a part of *Sanătan* Scriptures. The term *'Ganit'*, meaning the science of calculation, appears frequently in Vedic literature. A group of *16 Sutras* was widely used in *Vedic* times to solve arithmetic and algebraic problems, and now it is known as *Vedic* mathematics.

Mathematics or *Ganit* includes *Ank Ganit* (Arithmetic), *Bij Ganit* (Algebra), *Rekhă Ganit* (Geometry), and *Jyotish* (Astronomy and Astrology). Between 1000 B.C. and 1000 A.D., numerous treatises on mathematics were written by Indian mathematicians. The concept of zero, the decimal system, and algebraic techniques originated from India and reached the West through the *Arabs*. This knowledge revolutionized the scientific and industrial world.

The earliest book of mathematics is *Sulabhasutra*, written by *Buddhayan* in the 6th century B.C. In this book, there is a concept of the Pythagorean theorem and also Pi (the ratio between the circumference and diameter of a circle).

Around 499 A.D., *Ăryabhatta* wrote a book called *'Ăryabhattia,'* in which the concepts of mathematics and astronomy were explicitly explained. The book includes the decimal system, number theory, geometry, algebra, and trigonometry. He formulated the area of a triangle and provided a more accurate value for Pi.

According to his book *Aryabhatiyam*, *Ganitapad* 10; Pi is an irrational number (अपरिमेय संख्या) with a value of nearly 3.1416.

Later on, *Bhăskarăchărya* (12th century A.D.) also independently calculated the value of Pi as 3.1416 in his book Lilăvati-Sloka 98. The modern value of Pi is 3.1415926.

Ăryabhatta also worked on determining the position of planets and clarified the cause of eclipses. He stated that the earth is round and that the daily rotation of the earth on its axis accounts for the daily rising and setting of the sun, about a thousand years before Galileo was persecuted for making the same claim.

Ăryabhatta conceived the elliptical orbit of the planets a thousand years before Kepler in the West arrived at the same conclusion. He even estimated the length of a year at 365 days, 6 hours, 12 minutes, and 30 seconds, differing only by a few minutes from modern calculations. The translation of *Aryabhătia* into Latin in the 13th century significantly contributed to European understanding.

The contributions of mathematicians like *Brahmagupta* (7th century A.D.), *Mahăvirăchărya* (9th century A.D.), and *Bhăskarăchărya* (12th century A.D.) hold great significance, benefiting the world. *Brahmagupta* confirmed that all objects with mass are attracted towards the center of the earth and calculated the circumference of the earth to be 5000 *yojan*; with *yojan* assumed to be 7.2 km, this estimation is close to the accurate value.

The idea of nine planets revolving around the sun has been known in India for a long time, and Astronomy and Astrology developed due to their relationship with planetary movements.

The first book of Astrology is *Brigusamhita*, authored by the eminent *Vedic Rishi Bhrigu. Bhrigu*, one of the seven first *Rishis*, is highly respected by Hindus even today. Analyzing permutations and combinations involving nine planets, twelve zodiac signs, time, date, and birthplace of countless individuals, and deriving solid conclusions is an unimaginable feat. *Maharshi Bhrigu* and his son *Maharshi Shukrăchărya* dedicated their lives to discovering this profound theory.

In the *Gită*, *Krishna* says:

महर्षीणाम् भृगुः अहम्.., Gită 10.25

(I am *Bhrigu* among the *Maharishis*.)

He is regarded as the most significant among great *Rishis*.

Indian works on Mathematics, astronomy, medicine, science, and philosophy were translated into *Arabic* in the 8th and 9th centuries, and later by Al-*Biruni* (who came to India with *Mahmud* of *Ghazni* in 1017 A.D.). His book *'Tareekh al-Hind'* (The History of India) was written in Arabic in the early 11th century. Through *Arabs*, Europeans were influenced by and greatly benefited from this knowledge.

Ancient India is renowned for its proficiency in architecture, sculpture, metallurgy, navigation, and cloth-weaving.

CHAPTER 16
MEDICAL SCIENCE

Regarding medicine, the *Atharvaveda* (2nd millennium B.C.E.) is the first book where we find mentions of diseases, their medicines, and remedies. The book is known to prescribe treatments for about 99 diseases. During the *Vedic* period, *Ashvini Kumăr* and *Dhanvantari* were medicine practitioners and are considered gods of medicine.

Around 800 B.C., *Takshashila* and *Vărănasi* emerged as centers of learning medicine. Two important treatises from this period are the *'Charaka Samhită'* by *Maharshi Charaka*, which deals with the Indian traditional medical system called *Ăyurveda*, and the *'Sushrut Samhită'* of *Maharshi Sushruta*, which deals with surgery.

The *Charaka Samhită* describes theories on the human body, etiology, symptomology, and therapeutics for a wide range of diseases. It mentions 340 medicinal plants. The credit for the original knowledge of *Ăyurveda* goes to *Maharshi Atreya*, which was enriched and compiled by *Maharshi Agnivesha* and *Maharshi Charaka*.

About 3000 years ago, *Maharshi Sushruta* performed successful plastic surgery and is credited with performing many other surgeries, earning him the title of the "father of surgery." The *Sushrut Samhită* contains descriptions of 1120 diseases and 700 medicinal plants.

Historical information suggests that public hospitals were first started by *Ashoka* in the 3rd century B.C.E. Faxian, who came to India in 401 C.E., took an interest in contemporary health arrangements in India. He was very impressed by the health facilities available to the common masses in 5th-century *Pătaliputra*. He writes that all diseased, poor, and destitute individuals were examined by doctors and provided with every kind of health care they required, including food and medicine.

The *Arthashăstra*, a famous treatise from the 3rd century B.C.E, envisions a corps of physicians ready in the rear with drugs, bandages, and other equipment to care for the wounded.

Ăyurveda is a system of health care, both preventive and curative. It is an art of healthy living that has evolved through trial and error and analysis of the effects of numerous medicinal herbs on different diseases for thousands of years. Now, the world is realizing its importance with more sincerity, as seen in the increasing export of *Ayurvedic* medicines. About 30 countries in the world have recognised these medicines, and the number is increasing day by day.

Marriage among blood relations is prevalent in many religions and tribes, but medical science has now realised that such marriages increase the possibility of genetic disorders and physical and mental weaknesses. The *Rishis* had realised this fact long ago, and marriage among blood relations is strictly prohibited in *Sanătan Dharma* from time immemorial. The *Rishis* studied deeply and analyzed human behaviour, health, diseases, and remedies.

CHAPTER 17
RESPECT AND LOVE FOR NATURE

At Dubai airport, appreciating and advertising to enhance renewable energy, it was written on the board: *"We are all subscribers of the one sustainable world..."*

"The Indian way of life provides the vision of a natural and real way of life. We veil ourselves with unnatural masks. On the face of India are the tender expressions which carry the mark of the Creator's hand."

- George Bernard Shaw

Modern science is curious to know and look into the universe whose dimension is billions of light-years, which was created more than 13 billion years ago and has billions of galaxies with billions of stars. This is appreciable, but we are not paying sufficient heed to our planet, which is very tiny with respect to the universe. We do not pay sufficient importance to protect and preserve the pale blue dot, the only home we have. However, now the entire humanity is realizing the importance of the earth and its atmosphere. Man can live without luxuries but won't survive if we continue to go against nature. Harmony with nature is essential for the happiness and sustainable growth of mankind and all living beings.

Our *Rishis* had realised it long ago. They had care and concern for nature right from the beginning. Worship of nature was looked upon as uncivilized by the West, and Hindus were criticized as a nature-worshiping tribe. Modern science strives to conquer nature, but our Rishis desired to live in harmony with nature. *Vedic Rishis* were loaded with emotion, love, and respect for the entire creation, especially for the earth and its atmosphere.

It is amazing that during the popular *Shanti Păth* (Prayer for peace) in *Yajurveda*, the *Rishis* prayed:

"ऊँ वनस्पतयः शांतिः, ऊँ औषधयः शांतिः।"

(May there be peace in vegetation (plants, trees); May there be peace in medicinal plants.)

Rishis were aware that there is consciousness even in plants and trees, and peace and harmony are required for the survival and welfare of living beings. One of the main objectives of *Dharma* is harmony between man and larger nature. They have a special respect for medicinal plants because they are the protectors of living beings and the special gifts of the Divine.

In *Rigveda*, the *Rishi* prays:

"औषधीः इति मातरः तत् एव देवी उप ब्रुवे।" ऋग्वेद 10.97.4

(O goddess medicinal plant! I call you mother.)

Recent studies and surveys have supported the views of *Rishis* that residing in greenery and near rivers is beneficial for mental and physical health.

"We recognise that both green and blue spaces have a positive impact on people's mental and physical health. Our findings enforce the need to protect and invest in natural spaces to optimize the potential benefits to subjective well-being."

- A study team of Sapienza University of Rome

Protection of nature is our culture. Nature is considered a manifested form of formless Divine. There is an intimate feeling of companionship with nature with every breath intake. Thousands and thousands of years ago, the Rishis knew well the importance of nature and were loaded with emotion and gratitude. In Rigveda, many Mantras have been composed adoring mountains, trees, and rivers. They realised that living near nature has a better cognitive effect.

"उपह्वरे गिरीणाम् संगथे च नदिनाम् धिया विप्रः अजायत। ऋग्वेद 8.6.28"
(Residing in the mountains and near the junction of rivers has a good impact on the minds of learned persons.)

For enlightenment, residing in the forest is one of the essential factors.

"तपः श्रद्धे ये हि उपवसन्ति अरण्ये शान्ताः विद्वांसो...
अमृतः स पुरुषो हि अव्ययात्मा। मुण्डकोपनिषद 1.11"

(The learned man indulged in penance with a cool mind, full of reverence, residing in the forest... gets immortality and becomes imperishable.)

Lord Krishna established an ideal when he loved animals, especially cows; trees and plants of *Vrindăvan* and cleansed the river *Yamună*. He loved all, including human beings. He loved and respected even non-livings that are beneficial to humanity. It is said that He advised the people of *Gokul* to worship *Govardhan* hill, in place of god *Indra*, the rain-god, because the hill saved them from the damage of heavy rains and floods. Worship of *Govardhan* is still prevalent.

Krishna is worshipped as a love-God.

"रसो वै सः। तैत्तिरीय उपनिषद, ब्रह्मानंद वल्ली-37"

(Surely, He is delight and pleasure.)

Now the health studies by modern scientists show that people who live in green spaces have better cognition and a slower rate of cognitive decline. We have evolved with nature, and being an insepar ăble part of it, it is our natural setting. We are strongly connected to nature. Looking at nature's scenes helps us to recover from stress quicker. Exposure to greenery is also beneficial for eyesight. Especially, in the forest or in the mountains, there is solitude and abundant oxygen, pure air. Solitude makes the mind spiritually receptive. This is also the reason why residing in forests was preferred by *Rishis*. *Rishis* realised that nature brings better health, greater positivity, and creativity. So, in ancient days, *Gurukuls* (educational institutions) were established in deep forests.

It has been scientifically proved that plants have emotions; they feel pleasure and pain. Schopenhauer, a German philosopher (1788-1860), is of the view that plants and animals have will power. He writes, "The lower we go in the form of life, the smaller we find the role of intellect; but not so with will... The lower forms of life are entirely made up of will, without knowledge."

The researchers have, for the first time, found evidence of plants making airborne emission of ultrasound screams when subjected to stresses. The experiment was conducted with tomato and tobacco plants. They were subjected to two different stresses - drought and cutting of stems.

Worship of nature was looked upon as barbaric, but now, when the climate change is taking an uncontrollable destructive turn and threatening the very existence of the human race, scientists have realised the importance of nature. Now, the human species is under stress because non-human species are in danger. Everything, living and non-living, are interconnected in nature. Now we have realised that for sufficient oxygen, the surroundings must blossom with green plants.

For a healthy existence of human beings, the oceans, rivers, mountains, and the entire natural environment must be clean. We should show reverence towards nature and the earth.

Our *Rishis* recognised this long ago. They understood that the natural world is a community of living beings with feelings, which suffer or rejoice based on how we treat them. They referred to rivers and the earth as mothers.

Anything that nourishes and protects all beings is revered as a mother. The earth is the mother of all mothers.

"The earth, which offers us food, sustains and protects various life forms. May this mother earth bestow on us her beautiful gifts." - Bhumi sukta, Atharva Veda

माता पृथ्वी पुत्रोहम्। अथर्व वेद

("I am a son of the mother earth.")

नमो मात्रे पृथिव्यै। यजुर्वेद

("Bowing to the mother earth.")

This simple statement holds two valuable directions. First, we are all part of one earth and one family. Secondly, we should treat and protect the earth as our mother.

In the *Rigveda*, the earth, rivers, air, water, clouds, fire, and medicinal plants, all beneficial to humanity and all living beings, are respected and prayed to as gods in various Mantras *(Rigveda-1.159.1, 5.84.2, 10.97.4, 1.23.16, 3.33.13)*.

The significance and gifts of nature are sometimes difficult to explain scientifically to common people. Therefore, the Rishis connected them with religious practices, making it easier and essential to observe. Some trees have no commercial value, and to protect them, the *Rishis* warned that gods reside in *Pipal* and Banyan trees.

Krishna says in the *Gitǎ*:

"I am the Peepal tree among the trees."

According to *Skandha Purǎna*, planting *Peepal, Banyan, Neem, Bel, tarmind, Kavit, and Amla* trees would spare a person from going to hell.

These theories are effective, and even intellectual Hindus avoid cutting down green trees. Hindus respect all natural objects, especially those beneficial to humanity. Some conservative individuals from other religions criticize Hindus for their reverence and worship of the sun, moon, animals, plants, and rivers like cow, *Tulsi-plant*, and *Ganga*. These objects are called mothers because they have supported the existence of human beings since ancient times. *Tulsi*, a medicinal plant, has unparalleled ability to boost immunity and protect from diseases. It is abundantly available in all seasons, and these benevolent natural objects are considered special gifts of the Divine.

Being closest to Cosmic Consciousness is feeling the presence of consciousness even in every leaf of a plant. Take the example of the *Tulsi* plant, a medicinal plant whose leaves are beneficial and often plucked, sometimes daily. It is considered genuine to water the plant and bow one's head before it as a religious deed, acknowledging the frequent damage and pain caused to it, if one perceives its consciousness.

Protecting and keeping rivers clean is undoubtedly beneficial for humanity and other living beings.

CHAPTER 18
FESTIVALS ARE NATURE-BASED

Hindus choose to be celebrant, embracing joy and festivities that spread fragrance. They are nature-friendly.

There is a story about *Lord Krishna* who made the river *Yamună* pollution-free by removing *Kălia Năg*, a poisonous snake, residing in *Yamună* with its family. But *Krishna* did not kill *Kălia*; instead, he ordered it to leave *Yamună* and go to the sea with its family.

During the rainy season, there is a peculiar festival called *Năgapanchami*, which means a festival to worship snakes. India was known as the country of snake-charmers and has a variety of snakes in abundance. Some of them are poisonous, but most of them are harmless. However, due to fear, people tend to kill snakes, especially during the rainy season when water-logging areas increase.

But is it genuine to kill and finish the snake race? Absolutely not. Every living being should have the right to live, and *Sanătan Dharma* teaches us to see all creatures, including snakes, as part of one Supreme Cosmic Consciousness. Man, endowed with the richest wealth of wisdom, may be considered as the representative of the Creator on Earth. We should save them from being endangered and ensure that even snakes have their due right to live happily on Earth. Our *Rishis* believe that every creature should live happily, and nothing is to be rejected; everything has a proper place in the cosmos.

Snakes are also beneficial for the human race as they play an essential role in balancing the Earth's ecological system. They are part of the food chain, and man should not obstruct this divine system.

To save snakes is considered a religious duty, and there is a tradition to celebrate *Năgapanchami* during the rainy season to remove hatred for snakes.

The festivals of Hindus are often based on seasons or crops. There is a tradition not to celebrate marriages during the rainy season due to water-logging. Even saints, who generally move from place to place, are prohibited from moving during the four months of the rainy season called *Chaturămăsa* (चतुर्मास). These prohibitions are religion-based.

Towards the end of the rainy season, there is the onset of many rituals and celebrations to overcome the mundane life of the season. When the rainy season is over, there is moisture and dampness everywhere, and there is sadness and depression. According to medical science, there is less secretion of the happiness chemical called serotonin during this season due to inactivity and scanty sunlight.

This festive season also energizes the dull market caused by the rainy season, which benefits the business class and the economy of the country.

First of all, there is a ritual called *Pitri Paksh* (पितृपक्ष) in which fifteen days are prescribed to respect and pay homage to ancestors, forefathers, and *Rishis*. Hindus gratify and pray for the liberation of not only their own ancestors and *Rishis* but also the ancestors of devils. This broad-minded and all-embracing view is observed during these fifteen days when Hindus pray to God to bestow peace and pleasure to all the departed souls wherever they are.

During *Pitri Paksha*, there is a ritual to feed the crows, as there is a scarcity of food for them during the rainy season due to water logging. This season is also their breeding season and a time to feed the newly-born offspring. Crows play an important role in spreading and germinating the seeds of *Peepal* and Banyan trees, which are very useful for all living beings as they are good producers of oxygen.

Then *Navarătri* or *Dashahara* starts, during which Hindus worship the Deity of Energy, Mother of creation, to invoke spiritual energy.

"या देवी सर्वभूतेषु शक्तिरूपेण संहिता । दूर्गासप्तशती 4.35"

(O Divine Mother! You pervade the entire creation in the form of energy.)

Mother is the producer, so it is reasonable and preferable to conceive the creator of the universe and Divine Energy as Divine Mother, the Energy that pervades the entire universe.

"या देवी सर्वभूतेषु मातृरूपेण संस्थिता । दूर्गासप्तशती"

(O Mother! You pervade the entire creation in the form of a mother.)

Navarătri is celebrated to commemorate the nine days' battle and the victory of *Supreme Mother Durga* over a big army of demons. In the *Rămăyăna*, there is a story when *Lord Răma* worshipped Divine Mother for nine days to enhance his spiritual energy, enabling him to defeat *Răvana*, the symbol of evil, on the tenth day. Hence, *Navarătri* is celebrated to harness the infinite energy present in the universe, rejuvenate one's consciousness and spiritual energy, and triumph over the evils within oneself and society, the heaviness and lethargy of the body, and the gloomy thoughts of the mind during the rainy season. On the tenth day, at the end of *Navarătri*, Hindus celebrate *Vijaya Dashami* as a symbol of victory of good over evil.

Hindu scriptures always favor a respectful treatment for females. *Manusmriti* suggests and warns:

"यत्र तु नार्यः पूज्यन्ते रमन्ते तत्र देवताः।
एताः न पूज्यन्ते तत्र सर्वाः क्रियाः अफलाः। मनुस्मृति 3.56"

(When women are honoured, divinity blossoms there, whenever women are dishonoured, all actions, no matter how noble they may be, remain unfruitful.)

Vijaya Dasami is also celebrated to attach special importance to the feminine gender. This festival is a way to respect all mothers, human or non-human, as every female is a mother and a producer. Mothers embody love and sacrifice.

"विद्याः समस्ताः तव देवि भेदाः स्त्रियः समस्ताः सकला जगस्तु। दुर्गासप्तशती 11.5"

(O Divine Mother! Entire wisdom is your part, and all the females of the world are your parts.)

On the eighth day, there is a ritual to worship girls (कन्यापूजन). The girl child is respected with the belief that she is the manifestation of the Divine Mother. Some devotees also observe a fast for nine days or live on fruits and vegetables during *Navarătri*. This practice cleanses the body and mind.

Hinduism is full of celebrations that increase happiness, positivity, and enthusiasm. For example, when *King Răma* won the battle of Sri Lanka and returned to *Ayodhya* with *Queen Sita* after 14 years, *Dipăvali* was celebrated in Ayodhya to welcome him. Therefore, after 21 days from *Vijaya Dashami, Dipăvali* is celebrated.

Scientifically, less activity and sunlight during the rainy season cause sadness and health problems. To overcome this, Hindus celebrate the famous festival of light, *Dipăvali*. Light is a symbol of happiness and wisdom, and the celebration and illumination increase positivity in society. Every effort is made to clean the house and the environment, which can be moist during the rainy season.

After six days of *Dipăvali*, the festival of *Chhath* is celebrated in North India. This Vedic festival is celebrated on the banks of rivers or ponds, where the rising and setting sun is worshipped. Women wear colourful attire, sing folk songs of the festival while going to the riverbank. The festival's beauty lies in the rituals and offerings made, such as yellow and red fruits like bananas, oranges, apples, and homemade sweets, offered to the sun god and distributed among friends and the poor.

After *Chhath*, the winter season starts, and at the end of winter, when the sun reaches the Tropic of Capricorn (*Makar Rekha*), Hindus celebrate *Makar Sankrănti*. This festival is celebrated all over India under different names.

On the arrival of the pleasant spring season (*Vasant*), there is a festival to worship Mother *Saraswati*. She is depicted sitting on a white lotus with a book and *Veenă* (a musical instrument) in her hands, symbolizing her role as a *Săttvik* deity of art and wisdom. This festival is also known as *Vasant Panchami*. Generally, the new session of schools and colleges kicks off during these months.

In the delightful spring season, the festival of colours, *Holi*, is celebrated with enthusiasm, coinciding with the advent of the new *Rabi* Crop.

The Hindu New Year also begins in the spring season, when nature comes to life with warmer sunshine, delicate new leaves, colourful fragrant flowers blooming on dormant trees, and birds chirping gleefully. During this time, Hindus worship the Divine Mother, the Primordial Energy of creation, for nine days to elevate their spiritual energy and nurture their souls. Devotees observe fasting and lead a virtuous life. On the ninth day, called *Rămanavami*, the birthday of *Lord Răma* is celebrated.

There are various *Vratas* (religious observances) during which a family member holds a partial or whole-day fast for the well-being of another member. One of the most popular examples is *Rakshă Bandhan*, during which sisters pray for the success and well-being of their brothers, and the brothers promise to protect their sisters. There are also *Vratas* during which the wife holds a fast and worships deities for the well-being and longevity of her husband and offspring.

Vratas foster feelings of love and respect in the family, contributing to the strong bond of joint family systems and enduring conjugal lives among Hindus, in contrast to the broken home problem faced by some Western countries despite their prosperity.

Fasting is also considered a way of body cleansing and aids in healing.

Some rituals are personal, with individuals choosing to fast on specific days dedicated to certain deities. For example, some worship *Lord Shiva* on Mondays, Tuesday is the day of *Lord Hanumăn* while others observe fasts on certain days of every month, dedicating the day to worship and prayer. Some perform daily rituals, which provide clear objectives and a routine for disciplined living. Eventually, these rituals take on a spiritual significance.

Scientifically, medical science has established the benefits of fasting and maintaining a calm mind through worship. Fasting cleanses the body and reduces the risk of serious diseases like diabetes, blood pressure, and even cancer. These diseases are prevalent and challenging for humanity due to modern lifestyles and increasing stress. Worship also helps reduce stress and anxiety, serving as a source of healthier emotions.

Festivals like Diwali, Holi, and *Raksha Bandhan* are widely popular and appreciated all over the world.

CHAPTER 19
SOCIAL SCIENCE

About 2400 years ago, a famous treatise called *Arthashăstra* was written by *Kautilya*, also known as *Chănakya*.

Arthashăstra literally means economics; however, the book is more inclined towards political science than economics. It was primarily prepared to guide kings in acquiring and protecting their kingdoms. It is a *Sanskrit* treatise covering statecraft, economic policy, military strategy, international relations, welfare of the citizens, and the duties of a ruler. Some lines quoted below from *Arthashăstra* are still relevant today and worth following.

"The king should despise none but should listen to the opinion of everyone. A wise man makes use of the sensible words of even a child." (1.15.22)

"A king who serves with a rod (punishment) becomes a terror. A king with a mild rod is despised. The king who is just with the rod is honoured." (1.4.8)

Kautilya advises the king to seek the advice of experienced individuals. *"Therefore, sit and counsel with those who are mature in intellect." (1.15.21)*

He also emphasizes the spiritual learning of the prince. *"Therefore, the teacher should instruct the prince in what conduces to spiritual and material good." (1.17.31)*

Regarding having more than one boss, *"You should obey the orders of one who proposes what is beneficial to all." (3.10.39)*

According to *Arthashăstra*, *"a king should appoint counselors and listen to them. In the happiness of the subjects lies the king's happiness."*

Kautilya was a teacher at *Takshashila* University and the guardian and *Guru* of Emperor *Chandragupta Maurya*. He is considered a pioneer in the fields of political science and economics.

CHAPTER 20
FIRST REPUBLIC OF THE WORLD

Everybody likes freedom, the freedom to express and act. Sometimes, individual freedom and social welfare become contradictory. Our *Rishis* have tried their best to keep them in balance. In the *Rigveda*, emphasis has been placed on uniformity in thoughts and decisions in social matters.

The *Rigveda* states:

समानो मन्त्रः समितिः समानी, समानं मनः सह चित्तमेषाम्।
ऋग्वेद 10.191.3

(In meetings, decisions should be unanimous, and there should be uniformity in the minds and thoughts of all.)

Rishis emphasized collective consciousness, unanimous decisions, and unified actions. The election of kings by the people is referred to in the *Atharvaveda* (3.4). Although there was a system of kingship in ancient India, kings were not autocratic. *Purohit* (royal priest), *Senăni* (chief of the army), and *Grămani* (head of the village) had important roles to play in the decisions and administration of the state. The king administered justice and made important decisions with the help of *Purohit*. Great prominence was given to *Sabhăs* and Samities, which worked as checks to control the arbitrary power of kings. The words *'Sabhă'* and *'Samiti'* appear many times in *Rigveda*, indicating their importance. Prominent affairs were fairly discussed in these bodies.

The later *Samhitas* and *Brahmanas* (religious scriptures) also contain references to *Sabhă* and *Samiti*, which shows that they continued to exercise effective authority over the king. In *Satapath* Brahman, it has been written - *'Sabhă* and *Samiti* are the twin daughters of *Prajăpati* (king).'

The protection of life and property of the subjects was the king's most sacred duty, which also reflects during the oath taken by the king at the time of coronation.

According to the White *Yajurveda*, the coronation oath tendered by *Purohit* to the king is as follows: *"As a ruler from this day onwards, judge the strong and the weak impartially and fairly. Strive unceasingly to do good to the people, and above all, protect the country from all calamities."* The coronation oath taken by the king also includes - *"Between the night I am born and the night I die, whatever good I might have done, my heaven, my life, and my progeny may I be deprived of if I oppress you (people)."*

Vaishăli (*Bihar*) is believed to be the first republic in the world. It takes its name from *King Vishăl* of the *Mahabharat* age. He constructed a great fort here, which is now in ruins.

The *Rishis* also imagined a welfare state, which is similar to the concept of a modern socialistic state. Let us see the sublime thoughts of *Rishis*:

"स्वस्ति पन्थानुचरेम सूर्याचन्द्रम सा विव ।
पुनः ददता अघ्नता जानता सम् गमेमहि ।
ऋग्वेद 5.51.17, देवता -विश्वदेवाः

(Let us move unitedly on the path of welfare for all, like the sun and the moon, donating again and again, with nonviolence and wisdom.)

Upanishads contain a passionate appeal to the rich to share their wealth with the poor.

तेन त्यक्तेन भुंजीथा मा गृधः कस्य स्विद् धनम्। ईशावास्योपनिषद, मंत्र 1

(Enjoy the wealth with charity to the poor and nonattachment to the wealth. The wealth permanently belongs to none.)

The *Rishis* realised that the increasing disparity between rich and poor would decrease the gross happiness of society because the very rich would be in stress and the very poor would be in distress. This would defeat the purpose of the righteous ambition that all should live happily (सर्वे भवन्तु सुखिनः।). Modern economists and the government are realizing this truth, and rich individuals are being heavily taxed.

CHAPTER 21

ĂSHRAM, PURUSHĂRTH AND KĂMASUTRA

Everyone strives for happiness, but there should be a balance between individual happiness and collective happiness, between peace of mind and happiness, and between *Dharma* and happiness. Keeping these matters in mind, the *Rishis* categorized the aim of life into four parts - *Arth* (property, wealth), *Kăm* (desires), *Dharma* (right attributes), and finally *Moksh* (salvation or freedom from the bondage of the life cycle).

To achieve the above goals, *Rishis* desired to live for 100 years.

"कुर्वन् एव इह कर्माणि जिजीविषेत् शतम् समाः।"
- ईशावास्योपनिषद/मंत्र 2

(To perform these works, one should desire and plan to live for a hundred years.)

The *Rishis* divided the lifespan of a man, assuming it to be 100 years, into four stages, each one of 25 years -

Brahmăchărya (celibate studenthood) -

The first 25 years are allotted for *Brahmăchărya*. In modern terms, it is the student life, which starts at around 12 years when the child takes some vows for a disciplined life and is ready to leave home for *Gurukul* to study. This practice was followed in olden times. According to modern educationists, serious education of a child should not be started before 12 years.

The main purpose of the *Brahmăcharyăshram* is physical, mental, and spiritual development, and to develop the skills for the successful journey of life. The person has to strictly maintain celibacy, that is, to be free from distractions of the opposite gender, and get married after this period. Studying and gathering wisdom while sitting near the *Guru* is the main function. *Guru* means one who dispels darkness, and *Upanishad* means to sit near. In the olden days, even princes had to live in the solitude of forests in *Gurukuls* during this period. The *Guru* and his wife *Guru Mătă* are the teachers and guardians who take care of the students. In the absence of papers and printing press, knowledge was in the form of *Mantras* (formulae) and had to be remembered by chanting and orally transferred from *Guru* to disciples. Generally, the *Gurus* were *Brahmins* living in forests with minimal requirements, mainly met by begging and offerings from others. In modern days, this period is a time to study in schools and colleges.

Grihasth (householder) -

The next stage is *Grihastha Ăshram* (the householder), where one has to stay at home and be confined to family work. This period is from 26 to 50 years, during which one has to get married, and the main function is the all-round development of family members and taking care of younger and elder family members. These are the major tasks, and other responsibilities, like responsibilities to society, must not be neglected.

Vănprasth (partial renunciation) -

The third stage is *Vănaprasth* from 51 to 75 years when the offspring are supposed to be grown up and self-dependent. During this period, one has to take a step back from family responsibilities and be mentally prepared for the renunciation in the days to come. The main task during this period is the welfare of society and humanity.

Sanyăs -

The last stage is *Sanyăs Ăshram* (complete renunciation), from 75 to 100, which is considered the ideal age. *Sanyăs* means renunciation. During this period, the main task of the person is spiritual quest to gain freedom from delusions of the world. This is the period to turn within and start the inward journey, strive for self-enlightenment, cleanse the soul of impurities, and endeavor for salvation; search for *Sachchidănand* (*Sat*, *Chit*, *Ănand* - Truth, Consciousness, and Bliss). So, the task during the lifespan is the duty to the self, the family, including elders, society, and all living beings. The reverence and worship of ancestors, *Gurus*, gods, and God are advised. It is not easy to assign absolute dates to individual works. The *Ăshram* represents an ideal scheme and is not expected to be strictly followed by everyone.

For a successful life, what should be achieved is called *Purushărth*. As an art of living, *Rishis* have categorized the aim of life into four parts - *Artha* (prosperity, wealth), *Kăm* (fulfillment of desires), *Dharma* (duty towards self, nature, and all beings), and finally Moksh (to attain salvation, freedom from the cycle of life and death). All these factors are interdependent, and achieving them in due proportion makes life a complete success. Wealth is essential for a happy life. *Dharma* is required for the collective happiness of society and all beings. *Kăm* means desire, and no worldly objective can be achieved without desires. Even the universe has been created by the desire of the Supreme Power, *Brahma.*

सः अकामयत। बहु स्यां प्रजायेय इति। - तैत्तिरीय उपनिषद, बल्ली 2

(He desired, "I should be many.")

However, for salvation, which is the final goal of life, one must be free from worldly desires.

The *Rishis* contemplated, examined, and studied each and every aspect of life. They did not ignore even love, sensual pleasure, or human lust for the opposite sex, which is one of the desires and is also necessary for reproduction. The *Kăma Sutra* is the first book in the world on sexology written in *Sanskrit* by *Maharshi Vătsyăyana*. The book is dedicated to sexual and emotional life and love. There is controversy among historians about the period of *Vătsyăyana*. He was a resident of Bihar in the 2nd or 3rd century. Some historians are of the view that he was contemporary to *Chănakya* or *Vishnugupta*, the author of the famous *Arthashăstra*. Still today, the *Kăma Sutra* is widely considered as a standard book on human sexology and love. However, it is prescribed only for adults and is to be studied in *Grihastha Ăshram* (during adulthood) only.

CHAPTER 22
THE FORMLESS BRAHMA

It is said that a woman once asked Thomas Edison, *"Mr. Edison, what is electricity?"* Edison replied, *"Madame, electricity is. Use it."*

In the *Vedas* and *Upanishads*, *Brahma* is described as invisible, indescribable, and formless.

न तत्र चक्षुः गच्छति न वाक् गच्छति नो मनो न विद्यो न
विजानिमो...अविदितात्... कठोपनिषद 1.3
(Eyes, words, mind, knowledge, wisdom cannot reach there; He is indescribable.)

Then, how can we know His presence and existence?

We may use the hypothesis-method of science. In this method, what is to be proved is supposed to be true. If other facts related to it are in agreement with the hypothesis, the hypothesis is true.

For example, if we suppose that the orbit of the earth is circular, it cannot explain the other facts related to it. But if we suppose that the orbit is elliptical, all the facts related to the revolution of the earth are explained. Consequently, the hypothesis that 'the orbit of the earth around the sun is elliptical' is true.

Likewise, if we move ahead in our life with a supposition and full faith that an almighty, omnipresent super power exists, we will realize the efficacy, and his presence can be felt as a true guide, patron, and benefactor.

Energy cannot be perceived by the senses, so how do we know its presence? Its presence can be inferred by its effects. The electricity flowing in the wire is not visible, but its presence is known by the light or other effects produced by it. Even the light is not visible, but its presence is known by the visibility of objects in its presence.

Similar is the case of other invisible objects along with *Brahma*. Before the creation, there was void. In some scriptures of the *Dharma*, the Great Void is synonymous with *Brahma*. Void stands for the transcendental state of mind and the universe.

We can notice the *Mantras* in *Shaiva Darshan* regarding this.

शून्यया शून्यभूतो असौ शून्याकारः पुमान्भवेत्। विज्ञानभैरवः 40

(By becoming void due to the power of the void, one will reach the state of Pure Void.)

The presence of *Brahma* can be inferred by the effects produced by him. His foremost effect produced and realised by all is the cosmic order, which is amazingly scientific, harmonious, and judicious. He is known by the consciousness and wisdom present in nature. Actually, consciousness is the core of the universe.

प्राणो ब्रह्मेति व्यजनात्। तैत्तिरीय उपनिषद भृगुवल्ली 5

(Surely, *Brahma* is known for consciousness.)

येन प्राणः प्रणीयते तदेव ब्रह्म... केनोपनिषद 1.8

(Who arouses consciousness is *Brahma*.)

या देवी सर्व भूतेषु चतनेत्यभिधीयते। दुर्गासप्तशती

(O Divine Mother, you are known by consciousness in every being.)

Similarly, the *Upanishad* says -

ऋतम् वदिष्यामि। तैत्तिरीयोपनिषद्

(I shall call Him by the name of *Rit*, cosmic law.)

तत् तु समन्वयात्। ब्रह्मसूत्र 1.1.4

(And there is harmony and concord due to Him.)

Again, the *Upanishad* explains -

विज्ञानं ब्रह्मेति व्यजनात्। विज्ञानात् एव खलु इमानि भूतानि जायन्ते। विज्ञानेन जातानि जीवन्ति।

(*Brahma* is known by spiritual wisdom. By spiritual wisdom, the entire creation is produced and exists.)

"The design of the world is absolutely rational."

- *Hegel, a German philosopher*

Before the creation of the universe, there was void. In some scriptures of the *Sanătan Dharma*, the Great Void is synonymous with *Brahma*. Void stands for the transcendental state of mind and the universe.

We can notice the *Mantras* in *Shaiva Darshan* regarding this.

Om (*Pranav*) is the first sound at the time of the creation of the universe, so *Om* has become his symbol in *Upanishads*. Cosmic order, consciousness, wisdom, Om sound are effects due to *Brahma*, and these are the symbols of invisible *Brahma*.

Nothing can be his exact synonym or replica (न तस्य प्रतिमा अस्ति). Although the *Upanishad* states that He can be seen as a white light in the closed eyes during meditation.

अंतःशरीरे ज्योतिर्मयः हि शुभ्रो यम् पश्यन्ति यतयः क्षीणदोषाः।
मुण्डकोपनिषद 3.1.5

(By insight, He can be seen as a white light within the closed eyes during meditation by the *Yogins* of a cleansed soul.)

There are a number of Slokas similar to this in *Upanishads* and *Gită*. Like the *Om* sound, light was also produced during the first creation, so they represent him.

CHAPTER 23

AGNI REPRESENTS ENERGY IN RIGVED

"Great Agni, though thine essence be but one,

Thy forms are three; as fire thou blazest here,

As lightning flashest in the atmosphere,

In heaven thou flamest as the golden sun."

Rigveda (*Mur*-Original *Sanskrit* Texts, vol. 5, page 221)

Agni is not synonymous with fire in the *Vedas*. *Agni* is the visual form of conscious energy in the *Vedas*. It is one of the important gods in the *Vedas*, and its waves are all-pervading, like energy. Energy is subtler than matter, and in *Yagnas*, Agni serves as a medium between humans and gods. The waves of *Agni* symbolize energy waves.

"With its sublime, bright, and active rays, Agni pervades the entire space." Rigveda - 10.3.5

Discovery of Agni (fire) -

Great importance has been given to *Agni* in the *Vedas*. *Agni* is one of the gods. Out of 10,552 *Mantras* in the *Rigveda*, more than 2,000 *Mantras* are directly addressed to *Agni*. The *Rigveda* is the oldest literature in the world. The discovery of *Agni* or fire was the first basic step towards a civilized humanity.

In *Rigveda*, *Rishis* are credited with the discovery of *Agni*. *Rishi Atreya* says (5.11.6), *"O Agni, Rishi Angira sought you by his meditational power in the silence of the forest and realised the mighty power that you are; the son of the Energy, they call you, O Angiras!"*

It should be noted that the root syllable of *'Agni'* and *'Angiras'* is the same. According to this *Mantra*, *Rishi Angiras* has discovered *Agni*.

In fact, *Rishis* realised that *Agni* represents a mighty energy. The very life force of living beings depends on thermal energy. *Agni* is the source of thermal energy and light energy. In a way, *Agni* is a virtual image of God. Even the digestive system and the rain-cycle are the results of combustion.

Agni, the visual representation of energy, pervades the universe. It is pious and makes everything pious that comes in contact with it. It is considered as a medium between humans and gods, as it is believed that *Agni* delivers the offerings to the respective deities invoked in the process of *Yajna* and other rituals.

CHAPTER 24

DEVABHĂSHA SANSKRIT AND DEVANĂGARI SCRIPT

Rishis have a spiritual and psychological analysis of the communication of thoughts, ideas, and feelings. They have categorized the methods of communication into four parts:

1. **Pară** - Communication of Cosmic Consciousness to the mind when a purified mind receives instructions from God as intuitive guidance. This divine voice is called *Pară*.

2. **Pashyanti** - Communication from mind to mind. The word *'Pashyanti'* arises from the *Sanskrit* root *'Pashy,'* which means 'to see.' So, this can be understood as communication from eye to eye.

3. **Madhyama** - The intermediate unexpressed state of sound. Its seat is the heart.

4. **Vaikhari** - Finds expression in articulate expression orally or in writing, for which language and script are required.

The script used by *Rishis* is called *Devanăgari*. *'Deva'* means *'Aryan,'* and *'Năgari'* means 'intelligent or cultured.' The *Devanăgari* script is scientific. If any word is pronounced correctly, it can be written correctly; there is no need to remember spelling. Letters are called *Akshar*, which means imperishable. According to the theory of conservation of energy, sound is imperishable because it is also a form of energy.

The alphabet of the script has been scientifically arranged. They have been grouped according to the place of pronunciation. For example, the K (क) group is pronounced from the throat, the Ch-group (च-वर्ग) is pronounced with the help of teeth, and so on. There are five such groups, and the last letters of every group have a nasal sound, so each one can be expressed by the letter 'n' in English.

The letters beyond the above groups, य, र, ल, व, ह, combined with अं or म् or यं, रं, लं, वं, हं are of great importance in *Kundalini Yoga*. Chanting of these syllables activates and energizes the *Chakras* or spiritual energy centers of the subtle body. These chakras are considered synonymous with the plexes in medical terms.

Vowels - अ, ओ, उ, ऊ, अं, अः are also of spiritual importance in *Sanătan Dharma.*

In the *Gită*, *Krishna* says:

"Among the letters, I am अ ।" (Gită 10.33)

Lord Shiva says to His wife *Părvati*: "If one recites the great 'अ', O Goddess! the Supreme Lord arises..." *(Vijnăna Bhairav Tantra 90)*

Chanting of ऐं, ह्रं, क्लीं, which are often mocked in movies, holds a vibration of spiritual importance and is used in Mantras.

Hindi is also written in *Devanăgari* script with rare use of अः, but in *Sanskrit* अं and अः are of special importance. In the *Shabdarup* (word form of Dev), अं appears 5 times and अः appears 8 times. There is a scientific and spiritual reason for this. In *Kundalini Yoga*, Chakras (plexuses) are activated by pronouncing अं or म् or ओम्। In *Kundalini Yoga,* Chakras are the energy centers in the subtle body (सूक्ष्म शरीर), and in the physical body, *Chakra* is considered as a nerve plexus. In *Mantras* or *Sanskrit* prayers, अं or म् and अः are abundantly used at the end of the words.

Now, it has been medically proved that the sound by which the nasal area and the head vibrate is of utmost importance for physical, mental, and spiritual health.

CHAPTER 25
THE DIVINE SOUND OF OM

'Om' sound is also called *Pranav* or the first sound because it resembles the first sound during the creation of the universe. Hence, it has become the symbol of the formless, invisible creator, *Brahma*. At the time of the universe's creation, out of nothingness, three objects appeared - time, space, the golden embryo (*Hiranyamănd*); then bright light, Om-sound, and consciousness (Big Bang theory of science). These things symbolize the creator. They are the medium of the nearest approach to the creator or God because He cannot be visualized or described.

गिराज्ञानगोतीतम् ईशम्।

(He is beyond perception, description, and knowledge.)

The importance of *Om* is not only theoretical but also based on the experiences of *Rishis* for thousands of years. In the Gitä, *Lord Krishna* says, *'I am the syllable Om in Vedic Mantras.' (Gitǎ 7/8)* In the *Gitǎ*, *Krishna* is synonymous with *Brahma*. He is presented as the manifested *Brahma*, but He himself says:

ॐ इति एकाक्षरम् ब्रह्म... गीता 8/13

(Om, the one-syllable *Brahma*.....)

Om is the symbol of God in *Upanishads* also and a syllable of prime importance. Every *Mantra* starts with *Om*. Every *Upanishad* starts with *Om*. *Upanishads* are full of appreciations for *Om*. Let us see some examples.

ओमिति ब्रह्म । ओम् इति एतत् अनुकृतिः स्म। तैतरीय उपनिषद 1/8

(*Om* is God. *Om* is the only symbol of formless *Brahma*.)

एतत् एव अक्षरम् ब्रह्म एतत् एव अक्षरम् परम् ।
एतत् एव अक्षरम् ज्ञात्वा यो यदिच्छति तस्य तत्। कठोपनिषद 1.2.16

(Surely, *Om* is imperishable *Brahma*. Surely, it is the ultimate truth. Knowing this one gets what he desires.)

Lord Krishna says:

अहम् .. प्रणवः सर्ववेदेषु .. गीता 7.8

(I am *Pranav* (*Om*-sound) in all *Vedic Mantras*.)

All *Upanishads* wholeheartedly appreciate Om. *Mundakopanishad* (2/2/5,6) emphatically advises: 'leaving all paths, meditate on Om, this is the bridge to immortality..'

The sound of Conch-shell (*Shankh*) is of religious importance for Hindu rituals. Every ritual is started with the *Shankh* sound to remove negative energies because it resembles the *Om* sound. All *Mantras* also start with Om. In temples, domes are constructed to create echoes and resonances of the *Mantras* for more vibrations and effect. For more vibrations, अं or अम् and अः are abundantly found in *Mantras*. Dome-shaped temples are constructed to maximize the vibration of *Mantras* chanted in temples. When we chant *Sanskrit Slokas* or *Om*, the sound reverberates due to echoes and the hemispherical shape of the temple dome. The sound also resonates, and sound circles are formed, leading to better concentration and a spiritual feeling. In temples, bells also produce nasal sounds.

Guru Nănak says, 'इक ओंकार सत्त नाम कर्त्तापुरुष ।' (Aum-sound is the true name of the Creator.) In *Buddhism*, the main *Mantra* is 'ॐ मणिपद्मे हुम्।' *Jain Mantra* is 'ॐ नमो अरिहंताणम्।' We can see that Aum or Om is given importance in all religious sects of *Sanătana Dharma*. *Kabir* says: सुरत समानी शब्द में, ताहि काल न खाय। (If the flow of someone's mind enters the *Om*-sound, he becomes immortal.)

The sound of *Om* is the sound of the universe. It is also called *Brahma-Năda*. It is an eternal sound, the only unstruck sound (*Anăhat Năd*). *Om*-sound pervades the universe, everywhere, within and without. When the mind and environment are calm, *Yogins* hear a sound inside that resembles the *Om*-sound. The sound of fusion reactions that take place in stars also resembles the *Om*-sound. Recent research by NASA finds that the humming sound of the black hole resembles the *Om*-sound. The vibration produced by chanting *Om* in the physical universe corresponds to the original vibration that first arose from

Hiranyagarbh, the *Kăran Brahmă*. Hindus believe that all ancestors, gods, and God altogether are pleased by Om-chanting.

There are positive impacts of *Om*-chanting. The practice calms the mind and soul. Scientific studies show that chanting *Om* decreases depression, anxiety, and stress while increasing cognition. *Om*-sound results in psychological and physiological alertness, increased sensitivity, and synchronicity. It has helped many people suffering from Alzheimer's, dementia, insomnia, and Parkinson's disease. *Om*-chanting is beneficial in these diseases.

Scientists have recently discovered that the person who chants Sanskrit Shlokas has a better memory. The nasal sound of अं or अम् is abundantly found in Sanskrit, which sounds similar to *Om*. The Rishis intentionally invented and introduced it.

I am very much amazed and pleased to know that out of 23 Scripps National Spelling Bee Championships of the U.S., 21 were won by children of Indian origin in two decades. This may be a hereditary effect due to the better memory developed by our ancestors by chanting and remembering thousands of *Sanskrit* mantras of *Vedas*, *Upanishads*, and other Sanskrit scriptures when there was no printing press.

Medical science is of the view that plaques are deposited between the connecting points of neurons in elderly people, which are responsible for memory. The nasal and sonorous sound of recitation of *Om* and *Mantras* creates vibration inside the hippocampus, which is the memory region of the brain, helping in improving memory and removing plaques. Speaking *Sanskrit* loudly is also used as speech therapy for diseases like stammering.

Due to the deep humming sound of *Om*-chanting, N2O (nitrous oxide) gas is released from the nasal area, giving relief and solace to depressed and sad persons filled with gloom and despair. The nitrous oxide gas is euphoric and analgesic, which is why it is also called laughing gas. Stress and depression have become very common nowadays because of increasing ambitions and jealous competitions. If someone is feeling depressed, he should walk slowly and chant *Om* slowly; he is sure to get relief. *Om*-chanting releases nitrous oxide, and walking stimulates the brain, releasing feel-good chemicals dopamine and serotonin. At the same time, deep breathing occurs automatically, the health benefits of which are well-known. During chanting, if one feels the vibration, it is meditation, an important part of *Ashtanga Yoga*. *Om*-sound vibrates and energizes the *Ajnă Chakra* between the eyebrows, known as the third eye. This *Chakra* is associated with intuitive knowledge or insight. *Chakras* are part of *Kundalini Yoga*, which will be discussed in the chapter ahead.

Om-chanting also vibrates the pineal gland in the center of the head, which is of immense importance both medically and spiritually. It helps to produce a hormone called melatonin related to the sleep-wake cycle. The pineal gland is a mysterious gland at the top of the head, which is called the seat of the soul and is in direct communication with supramental levels, symbolized by the *Yogic* symbol of *Sahasrăr* or *Sahasradal Kamal* (thousand-petalled lotus). It is said to be the seat of *Lord Shiva* in *Kundalini Yoga*. The humming sound of the famous *Bhrămari Prănăyăma* resembles the *Om*-sound. It has become so important because of its enhanced health benefits and spiritual benefits. These facts are not imaginary but experimentally proved in hospitals. Thus, *Rishis* advise to chant *Om*, feel the vibration, and meditate on *Om*. *Om*-vibration makes the mind and environment serene and invokes the divine energy.

Om and *Shănti* are the essences of *Upanishads*.

'Om Shăntih' is uttered on all the auspicious occasions of Hindus. Praises of *Om* are abundantly found in almost all *Upanishads*, and peace of mind is the core of the famous Yoga. Every *Upanishad* starts with *Om Shăntih* and ends with *Om Shăntih. Upanishads* advise every living being, even plants, to be cool and calm and not to be excited. Harmony and peace inside and outside are essential for harmony in nature and society, and this is also the only path for the uninterrupted flow of spiritual energy from the Infinite Source to man. Both the syllables are of utmost importance in *Buddhism*, *Jainism*, and *Sikhism* too.

A natural question arises: which one is correct, ॐ or ओम्? Both the syllables appear in Hindu scriptures. But as I think, ॐ is the symbol of formless *Brahma* and suitable for focusing the mind during meditation, and *Aum* is suitable for chanting.

CHAPTER 26
FIRST GRAMMAR OF THE WORLD

First scientific and standard grammar *'Ashtădhyăyi'* was composed by *Maharshi Pănini* in the 7th century B.C., who is known as the father of grammar and linguistics. *Ashtădhyăyi*, a treatise of grammar bound by rigid rules, is the mother of all grammars of the world. This grammar was memorized in the form of *Sutras*, formulae communicated verbally by the *Guru* to disciples from generation to generation and was ultimately fully explained by *Maharshi Patanjali* (1 - 2 B.C). He was the founder of the world-famous *Yoga Sutra* and also the author of an important treatise related to *Ăyurveda*, medicine.

It is said that there were many grammarians even before *Pănini*, like *Maharshi Shaunak* and *Maharshi Katyănan*. The grammar was called *Pratishăkhy* (प्रतिशाख्य) in the Vedic period. Vedic *Rishis* had a scientific approach towards knowledge. Knowledge of worldly things is called *Apară Vidyă*, and that of transcendental is called *Pară* Vidyă. This is knowledge about the imperishable, who is none other than *Brahma*. *Rishis* had a scientific approach towards phonetics, poetry-writing, music, and they developed उच्चारण शास्त्र, छन्द-शास्त्र, निरुक्त. They were called *Vedang*.

There is a reference in *Mundakopanishad* (1.1.5)

'तत्र अपरा ऋग्वेदः यजुर्वेदः सामवेदः अथर्ववेदः शिक्षा कल्पः
व्याकरणम् निरुक्तम् छन्दः ज्योतिषमिति ।
अथ परा यया तत् अक्षरम् अधिगम्यते।

(Here *Rigved*, *Yajurved*, *Sămved*, *Atharvaved*, method of rituals, grammar, etymology, prosody, and astrology are *Apară*, and Pară is the knowledge by which the Imperishable (*Brahma*) is revealed.)

Inspired by *Vedic Nirukta*, phonetics was developed in the West. *Sanskrit* is a very old language, and many languages of the world have roots in *Sanskrit*.

CHAPTER 27

SCIENCE OF MUSIC AND POETIC TECHNIQUE

Almost all the religious scriptures, which are prehistoric, have been written in poetic form so that they can be chanted and remembered easily because there was no printing press in olden days.

According to A.L. *Basham*, a famous historian, in the 2nd millennium B.C., the priests of Aryans had perfected a very advanced poetic technique.

It is said that *Nărad Muni* introduced the art of music to earth. From an early age, music has been played at devotional and religious sites.

One of the four *Vedas*, *Săm Veda*, has been named after the syllable *'Saman,'* which means melody. It concentrates on the melody or songs. It consists of hymns and 1600 *Răgas* (musical notes) and *Răginis*. *Sanskrit* literature describes 120 *Tăls* or time measures for music. It shows how Indian music developed in the Vedic period. These *Răgas* and

Răginis are still important for the modern grammar of music.

The grammar of songs, instrumental and vocal music, and dance has been formulated in such an analytical, scientific, and methodological way that they are still prevalent and popular today not only in India but in the entire world.

Nătyashăstra by *Bharat Muni* (1 B.C. - 4 B.C.) is the first clarified and elaborated work on the subject of musicology in which rules regarding stage-acting, performance, gestures, stage direction, and music have been illustrated brilliantly.

In ancient India, many musical instruments like *Veenă*, *Vănshuri*, *Mridanga*, etc. were developed while these were unknown to the rest of the world.

The science of music called *Gandharvaveda* is counted among the *Upavedas*, subsidiary *Vedas*.

CHAPTER 28

YOGA - THE SCIENCE OF SPIRITUALITY

"Yogic methods, like the operations of science, are formed upon knowledge developed and confirmed by regular experiment, practical analysis, and constant results."

- Sri Aurobindo

The mind is the king of the body. It is one of the most sophisticated, finely tuned, and subtle creations of God. Science has developed technologies like E.E.G and F.M.R.I. to study the brain, and research in this area is ongoing. Brain cells communicate via electrical impulses, and E.E.G. (electroencephalography) is the test that measures electrical activities of the brain. FMRI (functional magnetic resonance imaging) measures the blood flow that occurs with brain activity. These machines also study the impact of different types of thoughts on the brain.

Medical and psychological scientists have found that a calm and tranquil mind is beneficial for human life. It is beneficial for memory, learning, decision-making, and positivity. It also helps control stress, anxiety, depression, and blood pressure.

"The link between stress and personal health, according to medical experts, is very strong. Research on the effects of stress suggests that a variety of stressors, including loneliness, academic pressure, daily hassles, and the lack of social support, can interfere with our immune system." (Cohen et al, 1992; Miller et al, 1999)

According to medical science, different states of mind create different types of brain waves, which are very important for physical, mental, and spiritual health. A healthy emotional state and a calm mind create slow brain-waves, which are rejuvenating and healing for the mind and body. The brain waves and nervous system are deeply related. In *Kundalini Yoga*, *Chakras* or the nerve-centers of the body are activated, most of which are located in the backbone. Therefore, the *Rishis* advise keeping the backbone erect and the mind cool.

Thousands of years ago, *Rishis* realised this fact, and in *Sanătana Dharma*, Yoga was practiced in different forms. While science has recognised the mental and physical well-being benefits of *Yoga*, the *Rishis* added an additional and important dimension, which is the spiritual benefits of *Yoga*. In *Sanskrit*, the root syllable of *Yoga* is *'Yuj,'* which means to unite or connect. *Yoga* is a connecting bridge between one's personal soul and the Super Soul, the source of unlimited spiritual energy. *Yoga* increases a person's receptibility to God's grace and Cosmic Energy. It is an art to realize the full potential of human life - a long, healthy, happy life, and other elevated transcendental achievements. *Yoga* broadens the inner dimensions, enabling us to connect with the Higher Consciousness and the all-pervasive consciousness of the manifest universe, and to live harmoniously with nature.

In India, *Yoga* has been practiced from time immemorial. Its description is available even in *Rigveda*, the oldest literature of the world.

"युज्यते मन उत युज्यते धियो विप्राः विप्रस्य बृहतो विपश्चितः।"
ऋग्वेद 5.81.1

(A learned person unites his mind and senses with the Super Consciousness.)

Even in the excavation of the *Indus Valley civilization*, we can find idols sitting in *Yogic* postures. In *Sanătana Dharma*, there are different *Yoga* systems. Even before *Maharshi Patanjali*, *Yoga* was being practiced to control thoughts, bring peace of mind, and attain spiritual upliftment. But the famous *Yog-Sutra* of *Maharshi Patanjali* is the most scientific, methodical, and best combination for physical, mental, moral, ethical, and spiritual development at a time for persons of all walks of life. *Yoga* is not religious but a spiritual practice. *Patanjali* is a great *Rishi* of the 1st century B.C.

Upanishads, *Gitǎ*, and many other scriptures have also advocated the practice of *Yoga*. *Mantras* 2.8 to 2.10 of the *Shvetashvatar Upanishad* are examples of this.

"दुष्ट अश्वयुक्तम् इव वाहम् एवम् विद्वान् मनः धारयेत अप्रमत्तः।"
- श्वे. उप 2.9

(As a wise master controls a savage horse of the chariot, similarly, a *Yogi* should control his mind.)

Patanjali made *Yoga* more scientific and practicable by categorizing it into eight parts (*Ashtăng*), the central and most important of which is *Dhyăn* (meditation). *Buddha* also emphasized it and used the term *'Samădhi'* for *Patanjali's* three parts - *'Dhărana, Dhyăn, and Samădhi.'* According to a recent study at Iowa University in the U.S.A., *Dhyăn* or meditation has a positive impact on the DNA of the person concerned. There are more than 100 methods of *Dhyăn* advised by the *Rishis*. Anybody can choose one or a synthesis of more, whichever suits them.

"'Chant Om slowly and connect with the following void.'" (विज्ञानभैरव 39) is one of the methods I like the most. Chant *Om* slowly and feel the vibration and the following void. By chanting *Om* slowly, due to long exhalation, *Prănăyăm* occurs, and by feeling the vibration and following void, *Dhyăn* occurs. *Prănăyăm* and *Dhyăn* are both vital parts of *Ashtăng Yoga*.

Now *Yoga* has become popular throughout the world since medical science and *psychologists* have also advocated the importance of a calm mind. In the modern competitive and ambitious world, stress and anxiety have become the main causes of so many diseases. In modern medical science, *Yoga* and breathwork are essential methods in *psycho*-spiritual healing for mental health and the all-around development of the personality. At present, meditation is being used as medication, and *Prănăyăma*, breathwork, as oxygen therapy.

"योगः चित्तवृत्तिनिरोधः।" - पातंजलयोगसूत्र, समाधिपाद 2

(*Yoga* is to free the mind from distractions.)

A calm mind is the main objective of *Yoga*. *Yoga* means to connect. When the mind is calm and undistracted, with pure awareness, the body, mind, soul, and Super Soul become harmonious, and *Yoga* happens. So, to control the distraction of the mind, *Lord Krishna* says in the *Gită* to be *Sthitprajna*, which is defined as:

"दुःखेषु अनुद्विग्नमनाः सुखेषु विगतस्पृहः।" - गीता 2/56

(Whose mind is not disturbed even in miseries or elated when there is happiness.)

"सिद्ध्यसिद्ध्योः समो भूत्वा समत्वं योग उच्यते।" - गीता 2/48

(Keep undisturbed in success or failure. Such equality is called *Yoga*.)

Neither disturb others nor be disturbed by anyone, advises *Lord Krishna* in the Gită. (12.15)

Among the eight parts of the *Yoga Sutra*, the first part, *Yama*, is for the purification of the heart and ethically disciplined conduct towards others. It consists of non-injury, truthfulness, non-stealing, disciplined character, continence, and no passion to acquire too much property. It is essential to mention that non-injury implies nonviolence in thoughts, words, or deeds. The second part is *Niyăm*, observance of disciplined personal nature. It comprises internal and external purity (*Shauch*), contentment, austerity (*Tapas*), study of scriptures (*Svădhyăy*), and self-surrender to God. *Yama* and *Niyam* support the peace of mind. If one doesn't observe these, it is impossible to maintain peace of mind. Similarly, if anyone is not in good health, *Yoga* is not possible. So, *Ăsan* and *Prănăyăm* are also parts of Yoga. *Ăsan* is to sit in a comfortable posture, especially with the backbone vertically straight. In a scripture of Shaiv

Darshan, it is considered an important part of *Yoga*. (For Hindus, *Shiva* is considered the Ădi *Yogi*, the first *Yogi*.)

Patanjali defines *Ăsan* in a very simple way:

"स्थिरसुखमासनम्।" - साधनपाद 46

(Sitting in a stable and comfortable posture is *Ăsan*.)

"*Hathayoga* introduced many light exercises and stretchings as *Ăsanas* to make the body fit and healthy, which is inevitable for the performance of *Yoga*. A healthy body is the instrument for all spiritual performances." (शरीरमाद्यं खलु धर्म साधनम्।) *Prănăyăm* (प्राणायाम) literally means 'a method of breathing.' *Prănăyăm* is roughly deep breathing. (These are not the exact translations). *Prănăyăm* is a very important part of *Yoga*. The importance of oxygen for health is well known. But we should keep in mind that only about 21% of air is oxygen, and normal breathing is not sufficient for ideal health.

In the *Gită*, *Lord Krishna* has dignified *Prănăyăm* when He says - *Prănăyăm is a type of Yajna (यज्ञ), an essential religious ritual of Hindus. (Gită 4.27)*

Medical science also appreciates the health benefits of exercise and deep breathing. Surya *Namaskăr* is an Ăsana (आसन) that is performed in the morning sun. It is beneficial as an exercise, and oxygen and vitamin D are also available in the morning sun. It has been medically proven that by exercise and exposure to sunlight, the mind releases a hormone called serotonin, which is a happiness chemical. The word *'Namaskăr'* (नमस्कार) stands for prayer. Many positive achievements are included in *Surya Namaskăr*. So, by simple *Ăsana*, the day starts with a positive mood.

All the eight parts of *Răjayoga* of *Maharshi Patanjali* are interconnected like body organs, and so they are called *Ashtănga* (अष्टाङ्ग). Each part supports the others. For example, during *Prănăyăma*, the mind is focused on breath, and meditation automatically occurs.

The *Shaiv Yog* System says, "By concentrating on the points of origin of breath, one acquires the state of fulfillment." (*Vijnăn Bhairav Tantra 2.24*). Again, the system brilliantly combines *Prănăyăma* and *Dhyăn* - "By practicing awareness on breath, there is an appearance of all being the same (Truth)" *(Vijnăn Bhairav Tantra 3.22)*.

As I think, to focus the mind on breath is the simplest and easiest method for meditation. Ishvar *Pranidhăn*, devotion to God, is itself a type of meditation with a positive thought and emotion that is reverence to God.

It should be kept in mind that *Dhyăn* or meditation is the most important and central part of *Yoga*. On the way to approach the Cosmic Consciousness, emotions and positive thoughts like adoration of God have an important role to play, which makes the path easier and also increases the spiritual power of the individual concerned. For an easy approach to the Divine, we have to develop both mind and heart.

Kabir Dăs was a famous mystic saint who had faith in formless Brahma, but he also gave importance to positive emotions during practicing *Yoga*:

"झरी लागे अटरिया गगन घहराइ,
गगन मंदिर से बरसा बरसे,
प्रेम मगन होइ साधू नहाइ।"

(Divine Grace is raining from the sky, a saint takes a bath in the rain with the mind engrossed in love and faith.)

Kabir wants to communicate that when the mind is calm and immersed in love and faith, Divine Grace descends, and the saint is drenched.

Kabir advises:

"संतों, सहज समाधि भली।"

He advises turning within and practicing a natural and spontaneous calmness of mind.

It is realised that during the modern age, IQ is increasing, but EQ is decreasing. Intelligence and reasoning are increasing, but compassion and empathy are decreasing. We should realize that man is a part of the whole, which is called the universe. The sublime sense of interconnectivity is possible when the heart is elevated with love and compassion. This sense of interconnectivity is often advised by our Scriptures.

In the *Gită*, *Lord Krishna* says, *"Those who are busy working for the welfare of all living beings achieve liberation." (5/25)*.

Again He says, *"The well-wisher of all living entities attains peace."* (5/29).

"The self-realised person sees Me, the same Supreme Lord, everywhere." (6/29).

Mahătma Buddha emphasizes compassion and loving-kindness (करुणा, मैत्री).

The three last and most important limbs of *Ashtănga Yoga* or *Răj Yoga* are *Dhărana* (धारणा), *Dhyăn* (ध्यान), and *Samădhi* (समाधि). These are three consecutive stages of the same process of mental concentration and parts of the whole process. So, *Bhagavăn Buddha* expressed these by only *Samădhi*. *Dhărana* is the effort to fix the mind steadily upon an object. *Dhyăn* is continuous and unbroken fixity of the mind upon the object. During *Samădhi*, the mind is wholly merged in the object. *Samădhi* has two stages *Samprajnăt* (सम्प्रज्ञात) or *Savikalpa* (सविकल्प) and *Asamprajnăt* (असम्प्रज्ञात) or *Nirvikalpa* (निर्विकल्प). In *Samprajnăt Samădhi*, there is consciousness of the object. In *Asamprajnăt Samădhi*, the distinction *vanishes*. It has been scientifically proven that when the mind is calm, the frequency of the brain-waves is less, resulting in the nearness to the Cosmic Consciousness.

Patanjali states that when the mind is free of dross and during *Dhyăn*, the nothingness appears, the *Samădhi* is *Nirvitarka* or *Nirvikalpa* (*Yogasutra*, *Samădhipad* 43). *Shaiva Darshan* opines - when one's mind becomes free of thoughts (*Nirvikalpa*), one becomes all-pervading in the highest state *(Vijnăn Bhairavah 31)*.

The state of nothingness can be described as the dissolution of the self into the Infinite. Oneness with the Divine springs in the state of no mind. *Lord Shiva* says to *Bhagavati Părvati*:

"विश्वमेतन्महादेवि शून्यभूतं विचिन्तयेत्।
तत्रैव च मनो लीनं ततस्तल्लयभाजनम्।" *(Vijnăn Bhairavah 58)*

(O Great Goddess! If one imagines this whole universe as being void, one's mind gets dissolved in it, and one becomes worthy of merging in that Supreme Void.)

It is advised to practice the thought-free state of mind and experience void and feel part of the Transcendental Void. In meditation, "simply being is better than doing something." So, *Lord Shiva* says to *Bhagavati Părvati* -

"By uttering the *Pranava* (*Om*) and by meditating on the void at the end of the protracted sound, one attains the state of Void (Cosmic Consciousness) by means of Supreme Energy of the Void." (*Vijnăn Bhairavah 39*). This is the beautiful blending of both stages of *Samădhi* and also more comfortable and easier to perform.

Ultimately, bliss and Consciousness are the spiritual quest. *Yoga* is a spiritual practice. When the mind becomes cool and calm and the soul is purged, the path to union with Cosmic Consciousness approaches nearer; we become more receptive to the inexhaustible source of spiritual energy or Divine energy. Man has been endowed with infinite potential. This is not only a theory but the result of practices and experiences of thousands of years of *Rishis*.

ते ध्यान योगानुगताः अपश्यन् देवात्मशक्तिं स्वगुणैः निगुढ़ाम्।
श्वेताश्वतरोपनिषद् 1.3

(During the practice of *Yoga*, one is able to see the divine energy covered by the *Gunas* during meditation.) The Divine often discloses Himself.

Lord Shiva says to his wife *Bhagavati Părvati*:

प्रशांते मानसे भावे देवि दिव्यौघम् आप्नुयात्। विज्ञानभैरव: 83

(O Goddess! One realizes the Divine flood of Consciousness in a calm mental state.)

Literally, *Yoga* means to add or to unite, to unite oneself with the Supreme Being or to add spiritual power to the soul; whatever you may please to say, but the meaning is the same. The *Yoga* of Patanjali is called *Răj Yoga* or *Ashtănga Yoga*.

There are different types of *Yoga* systems: *Bhakti Yoga*, *Karma Yoga*, *Janăna Yoga*, *Kundalini Yoga*, focusing on the common goal of overall well-being; physical, mental, and spiritual upliftment. *Yoga* is a method of mental discipline as an art of life for approaching nearer to the Super Power, to purify the soul, which leads us in the right direction, saves us from any calamity, and also brings enlightenment.

Different types of *Yoga* suit individuals of different nature and mental levels. *Kundalini Yoga* is popular among *Yogis*. In this method, there is an awakening of occult spinal centers (*Chakras*), which may be called plexuses in biological terms. These seven centers do not exist in the physical body but are considered to exist in the subtle body (*Sukshma Sharir*) as energy centers. *Sukshma Sharir* is considered the invisible energy field of the physical body.

The seventh *Chakra*, the thousand-petaled lotus *(Sahasradal Kamal or Sahasrar)* in the brain, is the throne of Infinite Consciousness. By specific meditation, a Yogi raises the level of *Kundalini*. When the *Kundalini* reaches the seventh *Chakra*, the Yogi gets enlightenment. This is a mystic method that can be practiced under the guidance of an expert *Guru*.

Janăna means knowledge or wisdom. So, *Janăna Yoga* means union with *Brahma* with the help of wisdom.

Dignifying *Janăna*, the *Gită* says -

न हि ज्ञानेन सदृशं पवित्रम् इह विद्यते।
तत् स्वयं योग संसिद्धः कालेन आत्मनि विन्दति। गीता 4/38

(In this world, there is nothing so sublime and pure as transcendental knowledge. Such knowledge is the mature fruit of all mysticism. And one who has become accomplished in the practice of *Yoga* enjoys this knowledge within himself in due course of time.)

Scriptures are of the view that ignorance is the cause of our bondage, and so knowledge is the means for liberation. The *Sănkhya Darshan* supports this system, according to which salvation is attained through the breaking of the union between *Purush* (personal soul) and subtle body by means of knowledge of the distinction between *Purush* and Prakriti. Then, *Purush* retains eternal isolation.

Philosophical support of *Janăna Yoga* has also been provided by great philosophers like *Adishankăracharya*, according to which *Brahma* is the only truth in the universe, and everything else is *Măyă*, illusion. What we perceive is not absolute truth, which is achieved through enlightenment.

When one becomes enlightened, the Truth is emerged. *Shankarăchărya* opines:

अहम् ब्रह्मास्मि, तत् त्वम् असि। ब्रह्म सत्यम् जगन्मिथ्या।

(I am *Brahma*, so you are. The world is fallacy; *Brahma* is the absolute truth.)

When we realize that the individual self is not the body but an inseparăble part of the Cosmos, the Truth appears, and *Măyă* disappears, and death also disappears. A healthy body is important as a medium to achieve spiritual wisdom, so it must not be ignored.

The aim and ambition of *Janăna Yogins* are enlightenment and to merge with *Brahma* and get rid of the cycle of birth and death by virtue of wisdom.

By positive emotions and sublime thoughts like compassion, devotion, it becomes easier to purify the mind and increase serenity and wisdom. So, *Adi Shankar* has composed many devotional songs for the deities. The *Bhagvad Gită* is an unparalleled scripture of transcendental and non-transcendental knowledge. The *Gită* is a great work that encompasses divergent themes of *Sănkhya Darshan, Karma Yoga, Bhakti Yoga, Janăna Yoga,* and *Răj Yoga*. It is best known for advocating *Karma Yoga. Karma Yoga* is not a part-time practice but an art of living the entire life-process.

So, *Gită* states -

योगः कर्मसु कौशलम्। गीता 2/50

(*'Yoga* is the art of doing work (mental, physical, spiritual)')

In the *Gită*, there is a balanced and beautiful blending between worldly affairs and spiritual affairs. *Gită* advises performing worldly duties and talks about the skill by which every action becomes *Yoga. Karma Yoga* is special in the sense that its purpose is also to check the tendency of asceticism, which is not desirable for society and humanity.

In *Gită*, *Lord Krishna* suggests -

तस्मादुत्तिष्ठ कौन्तेय युद्धाय कृतनिश्चयः। गीता 2/37

(Therefore, *O Arjuna*! get up with determination and fight.)

In *Gită*, the battle (*Yudha*) stands for the battle of life or action or effort, which is against asceticism.

Main philosophical support for *Karma Yoga* is the *Bhagvad Gită*. Deed is the cause of the bondage of the soul.

The solution is given in the famous lines of the *Gită*:

'कर्मण्येवाधिकारस्ते मा फलेषु कदाचन।
मा कर्मफल हेतुः भूर्मा ते संगः अस्तु कर्मणि'। गीता 2.47

(Only the performance is in your control and not the result. Neither carry the ego of the doer nor get attached to the result.)

There should not be a loss of effort or reluctance to action, but one should strive continuously. There is justice in the creation, and one is sure to get the due result.

So, *Lord Krishna* says:

योगस्थः कुरु कर्माणि संग त्यक्त्वा धनंजय। गीता 2/48

(*O Arjuna*, perform your duty equipoised without attachment to the result.)

Again, the *Gită* tells us that nobody can abandon work totally. Asceticism is not advisable. The behaviour of a person should be ideal for others.

लोक-संग्रहम् एव अपि सम्पश्यन् कर्तुम् अर्हसि। गीता 3/20

(Just for the sake of educating the people in general, you should perform your work.)

But, one should not have anxiety and lust for the result because this is one of the main causes of distraction, and there is no reason to bother about it.

मयि सर्वाणि कर्माणि संन्यस्थ अध्यात्मचेतसा।
निराशीः निर्ममः भूत्वा युद्धस्व विगतज्वरः। गीता 3/30

(*Lord Krishna* says: O Arjuna, Surrender the performance unto Me (Almighty) with full spiritual knowledge, without desires and ego, and free from lethargy; fight (perform). *Gită* 3.30)

Ishăvasya Upanishad is also against asceticism and advises to perform the prescribed duties and enjoy the property with some instructions.

In *Mantra* 1 and 2, the *Rishi* says:

'Desire and plan to live for a hundred years.
Know that God pervades the universe, which induces compassion and love for all and hate for none.
Enjoy the world without attachment to property because it permanently belongs to none. There is no other way out.'

Attachment results in ego and bondage of the soul, which hinders emancipation.

Next is *Bhakti Yoga*, the most popular and easiest for the common people. Spirituality is more an affair of the heart than the head. The sublime emotion like devotion smoothens the soul to reach near the Super Soul easily.

Bhakti Yoga is a spiritual practice focused on loving devotion towards God with auspicious attributes (*Ishvar*), which leads to proximity to Him. *Bhakti* is love for love's sake.

Sant Tulsidăs says:

हरि व्यापक सर्वत्र समाना, प्रेम से प्रकट होही मैं जाना। तुलसीदास

(*Hari* (God) pervades everywhere equally, but as I know, He appears by love or devotion.)

The *Upanishads* are also of the view that enlightenment can easily be achieved by devotion and God's grace.

तम् अक्रतुः पश्यति वीतशोको धातुप्रसादान्महिमानमात्मनः।
कठोपनिषद् 1.2.20

(One who is free from desires and anxieties can see Him by His grace.)

Famous devotee of *Lord Krishna* and poet *Miră Băi* was not a philosopher, but she was nearest to the Divine.

Rămanujăchărya (1017-1137), *Madhavăchărya* (1199-1294), and many more like *Rămanănd*, *Suradăs*, *Miră Băi*, *Guru Nănak*, *Tulsidăs* intensified the *Bhakti* movement. In *Bhakti Yoga*, the personal soul or Ătma does not merge with *Brahma* but dwells in close proximity to *Ishvar*, the God with auspicious attributes. The ambition of the soul is to enjoy the divine bliss, and the vicinity of *Ishvar* can be achieved easily through his devotion.

Bhakti took Hinduism far away from the formalities of Vedic rituals, austerity, and asceticism. It transformed the quest for *Moksha* into a loving relationship between the individual and his/her chosen manifestation of God, *Ishvar*. *Bhakti Yoga* is the simplest, requiring faith and devotion.

In the *Gită*, *Lord Krishna* says:

योगिनाम् अपि सर्वेषां मद्गतेन अंतरात्मना।
श्रद्धावान् वः भजते यः माम् सः मे युक्ततमो मतः। 6/47

(Of all *Yogis*, the one with faith who always abides in Me, thinks of Me within himself, and has transcendental love for Me - he is intimately united with Me in *Yoga* and he is the highest of all. That is My opinion.)

Bhakti Yoga is full of love and joy, enjoying the vicinity of one's favourite *Lord*. *Miră Băi* and *Suradăs*, devotees of *Lord Krishna*, are examples.

रसो वै सः। तैत्तिरीय उपनिषद् 2/7

(He only is bliss)

आनन्दो ब्रह्मेति व्यजनात्। तैत्तिरीय उपनिषद् 3/6

(Certainly, *Brahma* is known by bliss)

The bliss is easily available to a true devotee. It is never too late for a devotee. Ultimately, in the last chapter of the *Gită*, *Lord Krishna* says:

सर्वधर्मान् परित्यज्य माम् एकम् शरणम् व्रज।
अहम् त्वाम् सर्वपापेभ्यो मोक्षयिष्यामि मा शुचः। गीता 18/66

(Leaving all the paths, just surrender unto Me. I shall deliver you from all sins. Do not fear.)

Chaitanya Mahăprabhu, a saint of the 15th century, revolutionized the *Bhakti* movement with his *Kirtan* method. In *Kirtan*, one stops the mind from extroverted tendencies without effort, and *Yoga* occurs with enjoyment of music and dance. This is why *Kirtan* is gaining popularity all over the world.

In *Bhakti Yoga*, there are many branches, among the main ones are *Shaiva* (devotees of *Shiva, Părvati*); *Vaishnav* (devotees of *Vishnu*, *Lakshmi*); and *Shăkt* (devotees of *Shakti* or Goddess). Generally, deities of all sects are revered by all Hindus. Reverence and faith in deities are positive and the most important thoughts of people performing *Bhakti*.

In the *Gită*, *Krishna* says:

अज्ञः च अश्रद्दधानः च संशयात्मा विनश्यति। गीता 4.39

(Without knowledge, faith, and reverence, one can be deprived of his path and falls down.)

Maharshi Patanjali also emphasizes the important role of emotion in *Yoga*.

तीव्रसंवेगानाम् आसन्नः। समाधिपाद 21

(Deep emotions bring *Samădhi* nearer.) He means to say that deep emotions make *Yoga* easier.

The basic philosophical thoughts of *Sănkhya* and *Yoga Darshan* are the same.

एकं साख्यं च योगं च यः पश्यति स पश्यति। गीता 5.5

(Who sees *Sănkhya* and *Yoga* as the same, sees things as they are.)

However, there is an important difference. *Patanjali* introduced Ishvar *Pranidhan*, devotion to God, different from *Sănkhya*; an emotional touch in the process of *Yoga* which makes the achievement easier. Rǎj *Yoga* is a happy blending of *Sănkhya* philosophy and *Bhakti Yoga*.

समाधिसिद्धिः ईश्वरप्रणिधानात्। साधनपाद 45

(Success in *Samădhi* becomes easier by the devotion of Ishvar)

Ishvar is *Brahma* with auspicious attributes like kindness.

According to *Sănkhya Darshan*, any object is not required to fix the mind during *Samădhi*, but it advises a thought-free state of mind without the support of any object. Whereas in *Răj Yoga*, *Dhyăn* or meditation is an unceasing flow of ideas connected with one object or favourite Deity. The method of *Yoga* also occupies a prominent place in *Sănkhya Sutra*. According to it, salvation or return into one's true self is possible only when one's emotional stirrings are subdued, intellectual activities are controlled, senses are regulated, and the mind acquires calm.

In *Bhakti*, devotional songs are very popular. These are Yoga with emotion and enjoyment. *Bhakti* suits the commoners because it is the easiest way to deal with sorrows. It is full of emotions like respect, love, or affection. The devotee can approach the divine as a parent, lover, friend, or servant.

Lord Krishna says that He can be known through deep devotion. Gită - 11.54/55.

Maharshi Patanjali also advocates that there should be a presiding or favourite deity for the practice of *Yoga*.

स्वाध्यायात् इष्ट-देवता-संप्रयोगः। साधनपाद 44

(favourite deity makes the achievement easier.)

Temples are agencies for developing *Bhakti*. Deity's idol makes it easier, which are the physical symbols of the invisible and inconceivable God. The prayer generates emotions when there is somebody to listen to it. Emotion has an important role to play in effective prayer and being connected to the deity concerned.

It is important to mention that *Yoga*, especially *Răj Yoga* or *Yog*-method of Patanjali, is a balanced combination of transcendental and non-transcendental knowledge (विद्या and अविद्या) beneficial for the physical, mental, and spiritual health of a person. *Upanishads* tell -

विद्यां च अविद्यां च यः तत् वेद उभयं सह।
अविद्यया मृत्युं तीर्त्वा विद्ययामृतमश्नुते। ईशावास्योपनिषद्, मंत्र 11

(One who has both transcendental and non-transcendental knowledge, wins over death by non-transcendental knowledge and enjoys immortality by transcendental knowledge.)

In *Răj Yoga*, all propensities are suspended, and the devotion remains like butter by churning milk. *Răj Yoga* has become so popular that it is practiced by many people of all religions from almost all countries. The Noble eightfold path of *Buddhism*, including right effort, right mindfulness, and right meditation, is related to the control of thoughts and is almost similar to the *Yoga* system of Hinduism.

To sum up, we may say that purity, tranquility, faith, and serenity make the mind spiritually receptive, and we can tap the tremendous power of the Cosmos.

मन अपना निर्मल किया जैसे गंगा नीर,
हरि पीछे-पीछे फिरे कहत कबीर-कबीर।

(*Kabir Dăs* says: When the mind becomes clear of all dross, God-power arrives automatically.)

Faith and rationality are two ideologies conceived opposite to each other. But when they come together, there is revelation. As a conclusion, *Lord Krishna* says:

लभन्ते ब्रह्म-निर्वाणम् ऋषयः क्षीणकल्मषाः।
छिन्नद्वैधा यत-आत्मनः सर्वभूतहिते रताः। गीता 5/25

(Those who are free from impurities, who are beyond dualism, whose mind is engaged within, and who are always busy in the welfare of all beings achieve liberation in the Supreme.)

In the *Gită*, *Lord Krishna* again says that *Yoga* with faith and reverence is the best method among the spiritual practices.

'Among the spiritual practitioners, Yogi is better than ascetic practitioners, Yogi is also better than knowledge-able persons, Yogi is better than the persons engaged in work with desire. This is why, O Arjuna! become a Yogi. A yogi full of faith and reverence and devoted to Me is the best among all Yogis.' Gită 6/46,47

Maharshi Patanjali felt the need for devotion to *Ishwar*, which is an important positive thought to keep the mind cool and confident. The core point of all *Yogic* methods is peace of mind, but peace does not mean inactivity. Peace induces spiritual strength, positivity, a balanced approach, harmony, and clarity of performance and purpose of life with an unperturbed and undisturbed mind. This is why *Upanishads* and *Shrimadbhagavat Gită* never advocate asceticism. *Rishis* advise a balanced approach to worldly and transcendental knowledge and balanced performance in life.

For convenience, *Rishis* have divided the layers of the body surrounding the pure soul into five parts. These are called *Koshas* (cells): *Annamăyă Kosha*, *Pranamăyă Kosha*, *Manomăyă Kosh*, *Vijnănamăyă Kosh*, and *Ănandamăyă Kosh*. They are not separate but interwoven. Their right development is essential for the right development of the soul. They are parts of the body which are important as the ladder for the elevation of the soul to enlightenment. To enhance the inner world, the right development of the *Koshas* of the body is essential, which requires: right food, right breathing, right thoughts, and right wisdom.

The objective of utmost importance in life is to achieve glory in worldly affairs and establish proximity to the all-pervading *Brahma*, manifested or unmanifested in the transcendental world. So, in the *Taittiriyopanishad* (1.3), the *Rishi* desires: *'Let both of us (Rishi and disciple) achieve glory and Divine Energy.'*

(सः नौ यशः। सह नौ ब्रह्मवर्चसम्। तैत्तिरीय उपनिषद 1/3)

In *Gită*, *Lord Krishna* says to *Arjuna*: 'Therefore, rise, fight (perform), and achieve glory.'

(तस्मात् उतिष्ठ यशो लभस्व.. गीता 11/35)

However, we should be cautious about the distraction of the mind due to the desire for glory or prestige-consciousness. The desire for respect or admiration boosts the sense of ego, which is the last barrier to spiritual progress. For someone, the goal of life is to help people in distress.

"न तु अहम् कामये राज्यं न स्वर्गं न अपुनर्भवम्।
कामये दुःखतप्तानां प्राणिनाम् आर्तिनाशनम्।" महाभारत

(1 do not wish for a kingdom, heaven, and salvation. It is my wish to help in alleviating the miseries of the suffering of people.)

In conformity with the above statement, *Buddhism* opines that on the way to salvation on the seventh stage, out of compassion, the *Bodhisattva* willingly chooses rebirth to help suffering people.

The *Bhagvad Gită* has a solution - People with the above propensity automatically achieve the goal of salvation or proximity to the Supreme. *Gită* (5.25) states that the persons who are busy working for the welfare of all living beings achieve the ultimate goal of liberation.

CHAPTER 29
MIND AND THOUGHT POWER

"Perhaps in return for arrogance and spoilation, India will teach us the gentleness of a mind, the quiet content of the unequisitive soul, and a pacifying love for all living things."

- Will Durant, American Writer

"To love another is to see the face of God."

- Victor Hugo, French poet, and thinker.

Chemical secretions from the mind according to thought:

Wellness chemical - Dopamine, anti-depression;

Serotonin - mood enhancer, happiness chemical, released in daylight brightness, to see the brighter side of life;

Melatonin - a secretion of darkness, sleep chemical;

Endorphin - healing chemical, pain killer, laughing, playing playfully.

Alignment between mind and body -

There is a story of King Bharat who gave up his kingdom and retired to a forest for enlightenment. After some days, he was in meditation when he saw a baby deer whose mother was killed by a hunter. Out of compassion, Bharat became anxious about the survival of the baby. He looked after the baby deer and developed an attachment to it. At the time of death, his attention was with the deer instead of God. As a result, he had to take rebirth as a deer before liberation or salvation.

In *Prashnopanishad* 3.1, a question has been asked - 'how does consciousness enter the body'?

The *Rishi* answers:

मनोकृतेन आयाति अस्मिन् शरीरे। प्रश्नोपनिषद 3.3

(Consciousness enters the body due to one's will or mind-power.)

This is the power of thought. Thoughts are the building blocks of our life. Unaware of this vital power, we carelessly entertain all kinds of thoughts. Once we become aware, introspection and correction become easier. We should try to shed the gloomy thoughts whenever they appear and repeatedly call upon the positive thoughts. Happiness can be developed by simply practicing happy thinking.

The modern world has now realised the power of mind and thought and emphasizes controlling the mind through meditation or mindfulness, whatever we may say. But long ago, our *Rishis* were aware of the unlimited power of the mind. They advised controlling the mind, thoughts, emotions, moods, and rising from the position of a slave to a spiritual king. Every soul is eternal and all-pervading. The essence of *Sanătan* philosophy is to cultivate the habit of a calm and compassionate mind. The mind is overactive like a monkey and cannot remain empty for long. So, positive thoughts and emotions like kindness, love, compassion, reverence are advised. The thought waves are all-pervasive. They resonate with the waves of similar nature and return back with greater effectiveness. Positive waves return back with higher positivity, and the same is the case with negative ones.

So, in rituals, Hindus send the thought waves of reverence to God, gods, *Rishis*, ancestors, and have faith that the waves will reach them wherever they may be. The proof of brain waves is telepathy, which is realised by all. These are the only waves that travel faster than light. The effectiveness of telepathy or targeted brain waves depends on several factors like the degree of will power of the emitter and recipient, and emotions with which it is sent, and calmness of the mind of the recipient.

For a better analysis, *Rishis* have categorized the western mind into many parts like *Man* (मन, king of senses and production place of desires), Chit (consciousness), *Buddhi* (intelligence), *Vivek* (power of right-wrong discrimination), etc. *Yogasutra*, *Gită*, *Upanishadas* are full of ideas and the importance of mind-control. *'Vijnăna Bhairava,'* a book of *Shaiv Darshan*, has 112 methods to control the playful mind. When the water is clean and calm, one can see the depth. Similarly, when the mind is clean, calm, and collected, one connects to the Cosmic Consciousness.

Scriptures say that good deeds must be associated with good thoughts; otherwise, they will be futile. Let us take the example of charity to the poor. With a social and humanitarian point of view, this is appreciable and generous. But in the realm of spirituality, the thought in mind during charity has an important role to play. *Gită* says: if you are donating with hatred to the poor, the charity is *Tămasik*, and the result will be negative due to negative thoughts. If the charity is associated with ego and a desire, it is *Răjasik*, and the result will be worldly pleasure (*Punya*). And if the charity is associated with compassion, the result will be joy, bliss. Similarly, take the example of love. If it is erotic or with undue desire, the result will be anxiety and distress. If it is associated with a desire for equal return, the result may be worldly pleasure, and if it is unconditional and divine, the result will be divine joy. Even good deeds with negative thoughts bear negative results from a hygienic and spiritual point of view. In the spiritual realm, thoughts matter more than deeds. According to *Gită*, a man of ideal deeds and wisdom may not be free from bondage if there is the ego of wisdom (Gitǎ 14.6).

Again, in *Gită*, *Lord Krishna* says:

कर्म इन्द्रियाणि संयम्य य आस्ते मनसा स्मरन्।
इन्द्रिय-अर्थान् विमूढ आत्मा मिथ्याचारः स उच्यते। गीता 3/6

(One who restrains the senses but whose mind dwells on sense objects deludes himself and is called a pretender.)

Negative thoughts are prohibited because their harms are manifold. Negative thoughts like anger, jealousy, greed, etc., are poisonous for the mind, body, and soul. Their harms have been medically proven. Harmful hormones are secreted due to every negative thought. They disturb the mind, entire nervous system, and even the digestive system, respiratory system, circulatory system, and the entire body. Different types of electrical waves of different frequencies are created in the brain by different types of thoughts. According to the frequency, these waves are categorized as

Alpha, Beta, Theta, Delta, Gamma waves for analytical studies. The waves are recorded by EEG, electroencephalogram. Alpha waves are emitted by the brain when the brain is relaxed or in attention. Theta waves (4-8Hz) are emitted when the brain is deeply relaxed or inward focused (during meditation or *Dhyăn* of *Yoga*). Delta waves of minimum frequencies (<4 Hz) are produced during sleep, Beta waves of almost maximum frequencies (12-35 Hz) are produced during anxiety.

To sum up, we may say that when the mind is relaxed during deep sleep or meditation, the frequency is minimum, and when there is anxiety or tension, it is maximum. The more the frequency, the greater is the harm. So, sufficient and deep sleep is advised by doctors. But if the mind is excited when one is awake, the sleep cannot be deep. When one is relaxed during waking, the sleep is deep, and the brain-wave frequencies will be minimum, which will be beneficial for the body and mind both. The person who has developed the habit of living in anxiety may suffer from mental diseases like insomnia, and high frequencies are harmful to physical and spiritual health. A study by the University of California revealed that stress weakens the cell's structure, which increases the aging process. Some harmful chemicals are also released by the mind due to stress. So, we should be mindful of reducing stress to avoid premature aging and many other diseases like blood pressure, insomnia, etc.

Negative thoughts are also harmful from a spiritual point of view. With ill will, the person of negative thought loses some of his spiritual power. It may also harm the person in opposition if someone is the target. So, it has been advised to be peaceful and radiate peace to all.

Lord Krishna says in *Gită*:

अस्मात् न उद्विजते लोकः लोकात् न उद्विजते च यः.. यः स च मे प्रियः।
गीता 12.15

(He, by whom no one is disturbed and who is not disturbed by anyone, is very dear to me.)

Watch the thoughts cautiously. When the mind is dominated by negative thoughts like worry, anxiety, still your mind by forgiveness or other positive thoughts. Life can reveal its potential to the fullest when its vision is broad and all-embracing.

सर्वभूतेषु चात्मानं ततो न विजुगुप्सते। ईशावास्योपनिषद, मंत्र 6

(He who considers every being like himself does not hate anyone)

There is a complete alignment between mind and body. Negative thoughts are mental poisons. Allow them to dissolve when they try to enter the mind.

Bhagvad Gită opines:

समदुःखसुखं धीरं सः अमृतत्वाय कल्पते। गीता 2/15

(Do not be tormented by pleasure or pain. One who remains calm and indifferent to them is eligible for immortality.)

The *Rishis* always appreciated positive thoughts and emotions like love, compassion, devotion, reverence, affection, kindness, gratitude, forgiveness, or a mind void of thoughts. Positive thoughts have healing potency. Not knowing the power of thoughts, we carelessly entertain all kinds of thoughts. Listen to anybody with compassion. Look for things in life that inspire rather than infuriate.

In *Buddhist* literature (*Anguttara Nikăy*), the spiritual power has been mentioned as the power of benevolence, power of pity, power of cheerfulness, power of calmness of mind. This shows the way to spiritual energy just like Yoga. A quiet mind, touched by faith, is a good receptor of Divine grace, which is easily and readily available all around. Divine consciousness is present everywhere in abundance, to reach it is a mental phenomenon.

Tranquility of mind and sublime emotions are of utmost importance in Scriptures.

जितात्मनः प्रशान्तस्य परमात्मा समाहितः। गीता 6.7

(If one has conquered the mind, the Supersoul is already reached, for he who has attained tranquility.)

This also explains the famous teachings of the Bible -

'Finally, brethren, whatever things are pure, whatever things are just, whatever things are lovely, if there be any virtue, and if there be any praise, think on these things.' Phil. 4.8

Upanishads advise that be free from ego and treat yourself as a divine observer, and you are only a witness. Because when thoughts occupy the mind, they enter the subconscious and ultimately leave their imprint on the soul, which creates bondage for the soul and hinders salvation, the ultimate goal of the soul. As a conclusion, we may say that the happiness of life depends mostly on the quality of our thoughts.

CHAPTER 30
THIRD EYE AND AURA

Science is also envisioning the experimental proof of the third eye. The third eye, or sixth sense, can be realised in day-to-day life, more vividly in animals. During tsunamis, animals can sense the danger earlier and save their lives, while there is often harm to human lives. For instance, if you leave a puppy on the stairs, it will not attempt to come down because it can visualize the consequences. However, this is not the case with a human child who might try to come down and fall.

There are stories of animals displaying off-sight knowledge, such as an elephant refusing to cross a weak bridge in Europe, even though many men and horses were crossing it. Additionally, there are stories of dogs becoming sad and restless when their masters were killed in an airplane crash hundreds of miles away.

In *Sanātan Dharma*, there has been a concept of the third eye or sixth sense, which can be developed through *Yoga*. The sixth sense represents superhuman powers like intuitive abilities, omniscience, and the ability to know the past and future. The special methods to activate these powers have been suggested in Chapter *Vibhutipăd* of *Yogasutra*. However, *Maharshi Patanjali* warns that the ultimate goal of Yoga, which is *Kaivalya* or salvation, may be hindered by the desire and attempt to achieve these powers. Nevertheless, these powers are automatically achieved along with enlightenment in the long run.

The depiction of *Lord Shiva* with the third eye on His forehead is well-known, and *Jainism* also accepts that every soul has the potential to become a Super Soul. Jains, Hindus, and *Buddhists* believe that in the advanced stage during the journey to the Super Soul, an individual reaches a stage when they become *Trikăladarshi*, meaning they know the past, present, and future. In *Buddhism*, this stage is reached in the seventh stage of *Boddhisatva*.

The activation of the third eye occurs when the soul becomes clean and free of impurities, which can be achieved through different paths of *Yoga*. According to *Kundalini Yoga*, when the *Ăjnă Chakra*, located between the eyebrows, is energized through *Yoga* and elevated consciousness, the third eye is activated. The third eye also indicates insight or transcendental knowledge.

The *Gită* states:

ब्रह्मभूतः प्रसन्नात्मा न शोचति न कांक्षति ।
समः सर्वेषु भूतेषु मद्भक्तिं लभते पराम्। गीता 18.54

(One who lives happily with no anxiety and desire, disposed equally towards every living being and is devoted to Me (God) attains the transcendental stage.)

Sanātan Dharma talks about *Sukshma Sharir*, the subtle body, and *Prabhă Mandal*, which may be called the aura.

Presently, science is also trying to understand this concept. The aura is conceived as an energy field around the physical body of a living being. When we approach a living being, we are influenced by their aura, *Prabhă Mandal*, or energy field. The quality and influence of the aura depend on the quality of the soul concerned.

When living beings approach each other closely, their auras interact and influence one another. This is why Satsang or good company has been advised in religious scriptures. If we visit a great soul, we can feel the intensity of the influence of their aura. Generally, it is said that plants and animals have a purer and cleaner aura than a normal human being because humans are of a more complex nature due to better IQ and exposure. Hence, *Rishis* preferred to live near plants in the solitude of forests, and *Bhagavăn Buddha* attained enlightenment beneath a Peepal tree.

In the modern age, Kirlian photography is believed to capture the aura as an egg-shaped energy field surrounding the physical body. The photograph of the aura displays light colours. For example, if a person is sitting erect, the colour of the aura from bottom to top is red, orange, yellow, green, indigo, and purple. This sequence of colours is comparăble to and in the same order as the *Chakras* of *Kundalini Yoga*, signifying the energy centers of the subtle body. These colours are sequentially arranged from higher frequency to lower frequency, similar to the rainbow. This confirms the similarity between the photograph of the aura and the subtle body described by *Sanātan* scriptures long ago.

CHAPTER 31

GUNAS (SAT, RAJ, TAM) AS THE CONSTITUENT ELEMENTS OF PRAKRITI

Sănkhya Philosophy is a dualistic philosophy, according to which the universe is made up of *Purush* (soul) and *Prakriti* (nature), both are eternal, that is without beginning and end. *'Prakriti'* means that which is primary. It arises from the roots *'Pra'* (before) and *'Kriti'* means creation. The *Prakriti* of the *Sănkhya* is not the material substance. It gives rise not only to the five elements of the material universe but also the psychical. The development of *Prakriti* arises by means of its three constituent powers, or *Gunas*. Three *Gunas* - *Sattva*, *Rajas*, and *Tamas* are the constituent elements of *Prakriti. Sănkhya Darshan* of *Maharshi Kapil* is one of the oldest Indian philosophies, and it is a scientific philosophy appreciated even by Western philosophers. We have not to enter into the deep philosophy of *Sănkhya* but the three *gunas* of *Prakriti* which are very useful for every aspect of human life; philosophical, social, or behavioural. They are of great significance for the art of life of any man working in any field. The *Gunas* easily and scientifically analyze every strata of society and every stand of life.

Three *Gunas* are *Sattva*, *Rajas*, and *Tamas*. *Sattva* stands for truth, peace, purity, light, bliss, goodness; *Rajas* stands for motion, activity, passion, physical power; and *Tamas* stands for darkness, inertia, inertness, inactivity, sloth, indifference.

All beings have all the *Gunas*, but their proportion makes the difference. *Gunas* are the actual ingredients of *Prakriti*; material and psychical. *Gunas* are the constituent elements of Prakriti and cause of the bondage of *Purus* (soul). An interesting question arises - if *Satoguna* creates wisdom, peace, purity; how it can be the cause of bondage for the soul?

Gită says: it is due to the ego or attitude for the above attributes. Gită (14.6)

A detailed description of *Gunas* has been given in the 14th chapter of *Gită*.

Conducts, minds, thoughts, emotions, desires, feelings, foods, colours, all the internal and external contents of Prakriti, which affect life, are categorized among *Gunas*. The *Gunas* make the whole world evolved out of *Prakriti*. They are conjoined in varying proportions. If a man is *Sătvik*, it means that Satoguna is dominating in his personality. A *Brăhmin* or a scholar has to be of *Sătvik Vritti*, feelings, and desires *Sătvik*, eating *Sătvik* foods, living style *Sătvik*, dressing *Sătvik*, the entire environment *Sătvik*. Similarly, a person in administration has to be dominated by *Răjasik* propensity, loving energy, motion, activity, etc. So, *Krishna* says in *Gită* that I have created the *Varnas*, *Brăhman*, *Kshatriya*, *Vaishya*, *Shudra* on the basis of *Gunas*.

चतुर्वर्णं मया सृष्टं गुणकर्मविभागशः। गीता 4.13

Meaning - (Four *Varnas* have been created by Me according to the *Gunas* and professions.)

Later on, the division was developed based on birth and became almost hereditary.

According to the *Upanishad*, one who is learned is a *Brăhmin*. Teaching and studying are *Sătvik* professions, and so anybody engaged in it has to live in a *Sătvik* way, for example, he cannot eat meat because it is not *Sătvik* food. He should prefer a peaceful life with few desires and requirements. The persons who are in administration or the army will be *Kshatriya* dominated by *Rajogun*, and his living, food, etc. should be *Rajoguni*. For example, he was allowed to eat meat and other food that increases passion. Similarly, the persons engaged in agriculture or business are also in the same category. The rest of the persons who are dull with no knowledge and ability, engaged in the physical service of society are Sudras.

The devotion to deities is also of three types; *Sătvik*, *Răjasik*, and *Tămasik*; and so, the deity of Absolute Power has also three forms - *Sarasvati* is a *Sătvik* goddess generally worshipped by knowledge-seekers; *Lakshmi*, the *Răjasik* goddess generally worshiped by businessmen. When a man is ready to set out for war, he prays to *Kăli*, a Tămasik goddess because he may be compelled to kill even men, in this situation he cannot pray to Sarasvati. Action and intellect are imbued with *Gunas*. All *Gunas* are present together in an ever-changing ratio, one of them in a dominating situation. There should be harmony among the *Gunas*, thought, and conduct, each should be dominated by the same *Guna*. The *Guna* of diet is also important. Anyone with *Sătvik* conduct must have a *Sătvik* diet and so on.

Sătvik diet calms the mind, and *Răjasik* diet excites the mind. If one takes a *Tămasik* diet, it results in inactivity, negligence, and the failure of any action. Food affects the mind, and the mind controls the conduct.

So, in *Bhagvad Gită*, it has been advised:

युक्त आहार विहारस्य युक्त चेष्टस्य कर्मसु।
युक्त स्वप्न अवबोधस्य योगो भवति दुःखहा। गीता 6.17

(If one is regulated in diet, recreation, sleeping, and work, all pains are mitigated by practicing Yoga.)

A spiritual man has been advised to take a *Sătvik* meal. Diet is of immense importance, especially for spiritual seekers, in *Upanishads*.

Chhandogya Upanishad states:

आहारशुद्धौ सत्त्वशुद्धिः, सत्त्वशुद्धौ ध्रुव स्मृतिः,
स्मृतिलाभे सर्वग्रंथीनाम् विप्रमोक्षः। छंदोज्ञ उपनिषद 7.26.2

(When the food is pure, *Sătvik*, the essence of nature becomes pure; when nature becomes pure, the mind becomes stable; then the person concerned becomes free from all knots, ties.)

Rishis emphasized *Sătvik* food for good health for the common man. Now the world is realizing the importance of vegetarian food, which is mostly *Sătvik* if taken lightly and fresh.

Harmony among profession, action, conduct, style of living, and the entire atmosphere is essential for success. This is a scientific method to increase the efficiency of a man. I am giving you a suitable example from history. As I think, the main cause of the collapse of the *Maurya* dynasty and *Dărăsikoh*, the son of Shăh Jahăn, was the mismatch of Gunas of the aim, profession, and lifestyle. Their profession was *Răjasik* while they followed *Sătvik* lifestyle. After *Ashoka*, *Mauryans* had adopted *Buddhism*, which recommends nonviolence and the ruler of the dynasty turned out to be less enthusiastic. Similar is the case of *Dărăsikoh* who had no interest in warfare. He was interested in studying religious books. If one's intellect is *Sătvik*, it also reflects in his action. With no interest in the skill of warfare, *Dără* was defeated and killed by his rival brother *Aurangzeb*. Ultimately, *Mauryans* and *Dărăsikoh* failed in their lives.

In olden days, in Indian culture, the Kings were advised by *Kulgurus* in important matters and decisions because kingship is a *Răjasik* work that is dominated by passion, and their decisions may be wrong due to mental agitation. *Kulgurus*, being *Sătvik*, were cool and calm, so their advice was respected. Politics and religion were kept aloof. King Răma was an ideal man, but no religious book was written by him. There are philosophical preachings of his *Guru Vashishta*. He is credited as the chief author of Mandal 7 of *Rigveda*. He is also the author of a famous philosophical book *'Yog Vashistha'*.

Krishna had to play many roles in life, as a king and as a preacher. This is why, in the great war of *Mahăbhărat*, *Krishna* vowed to give up arms before preaching *Gită* to *Arjuna* because as an active participant in the war, his mind may be agitated, and an agitated mind is not suitable for philosophical preachings.

Gunas are the constituent elements of external and internal nature, and they also create bondage to the soul (*Purush*). *Gunas* interact among themselves and influence one another. The man who understands this mystery is liberated. *Gită* 3.28

In *Gită*, even *Dăn* (charity) is categorized among *Gunas*. If one donates with compassion, without any desire, to a suitable man, in a suitable place and time, it is Sătvik charity.

If one donates for a return or with a desire, like prestige, etc., it is *Răjasik*; and if one donates with scorn or insult to a person who is undesirable, and if the time and place are not suitable, then the donation is Tămasik. Similarly, diet, *Yajna* (oblation), *Tapa* (penance) have also been categorized among *Gunas*. (*Gită*, ch.17)

The result of *Satva* is pleasure; that of *Rajas* is engagement in work, action, and the result of *Tamas* is idleness, negligence. (*Gită* 14.9)

CHAPTER 32
VISION AND CONTEMPLATION

There is a story in the *Bhagavat Purăna* about an attack on *Dvărika*, the kingdom of *Lord Krishna*. Salva was a friend of *Shishupăl*. Upon learning that *Krishna* had killed *Shishupăl*, *Salva* resolved to seek revenge. He renounced his kingdom and worshiped *Lord Shiva* for many years. Pleased with his devotion, *Shiva* granted him a flying vehicle, a *Vimăn* named *Shaubha*, which was as swift as lightning and equipped with various weapons, responding to *Salva's* thoughts. *Shaubha* could navigate through air, water, and land with ease. *Shaubha* bombarded *Dvărika* but was ultimately destroyed by *Krishna's Chakra Sudarshan*.

Some individuals may view this story as imaginative. Nevertheless, the visualization is intriguing from scientific and realistic perspectives. It bears resemblance to modern drones, although it exceeded drones as it was controlled by its master's brain waves. In today's era of artificial intelligence (A.I.), such possibilities are conceivable.

In the *Rămăyăna's* narrative, we've encountered the *Pushpak Vimăn*. Furthermore, a treatise called the

"*Vaimanik Shăstra*" (technology of spacecraft) authored by *Rishi Bhărdvăj* remains available to this day. *Bhărdvăj* was an ancient sage mentioned in the Rigveda, the oldest known human civilization text. He was also the father of *Guru* Droan from the *Mahăbhărat.*

During the *Mahăbhărat* war, Sanjay sat in a palace at a distance from the battlefield, relaying real-time updates of the conflict to the blind king *Dhritarăshtra*, much akin to contemporary TV commentary.

Another instance is the *Mahăbhărat's* account of the birth of a hundred *Kauravas* through cloning.

While modern scientists estimate the age of the universe to be approximately 14 billion years, the *Rishis'* calculations don't align exactly but are also in the billions of years.

"सहस्र युग पर्वन्तम् अहः यत् ब्रह्मणः विदुः ।
रात्रिम् युग सहस्रान्ताम् ते अहोरात्र विदः जनाः।" - गीता 8/17

(A thousand *Yugas* constitute one day of *Brahmă*, and the same duration applies to one night.)

After a hundred such years, *Brahmă's* demise triggers the end of creation. This duration's calculation amounts to billions of years.

This perspective contrasts with the conventional Western belief that the world came into existence just over six thousand years ago. The *Rishis'* insight isn't unscientific or irrational.

Since time immemorial, Hindu scriptures have cautioned that bad deeds could lead one to descend from the human life-cycle, necessitating rebirth into a lower species and cycling through 84 lakh species from life to life. References to the 84 lakh species (*Yoni*) are found in the *Purănas*. Interestingly, today's number of species nearly matches this figure. According to Hindu mythology, Earth's plant and animal species total 8.4 million, which closely corresponds to modern scientific estimates of around 8.7 million.

Though I cannot confirm whether the *Rishis* calculated this, it astonishingly aligns with modern calculations.

CHAPTER 33
CRITICISM OF SANĂTAN DHARMA

Sanătan Dharma is an ancient tradition without a definitive beginning, evolving continuously over thousands of years through the contributions of numerous *Rishis*, thinkers, and philosophers. It encompasses a vast collection of scriptures that contain wisdom in diverse forms, including transcendental and non-transcendental, philosophy, history, moral teachings, science, and more. This expansive nature makes it susceptible to both moral scrutiny and appreciation. While it's somewhat normal for individuals of other faiths to criticize Hinduism to assert the superiority of their own beliefs, it becomes disconcerting when Hindus themselves criticize *Sanătan Dharma.* This is particularly disheartening when knowledgeable Hindus intentionally disparăge a profound religion like *Sanătan Dharma*, indicating not only a lack of familiarity with revered texts like the *Bhagvad Gită* and *Upanishads* but also a broader lack of understanding.

An essential point to emphasize is that Hinduism is characterized by its receptiveness to reasoning and questioning, in contrast to certain other religions. However, such inquiries should be focused on the philosophical aspects of the *Dharma*, such as the *Upanishads*, *Gită*, *Brahmasutra*, and the various philosophical schools of India.

To distinguish between the *Upanishads* and *Purănas*, let's consider the creation of the universe. According to the *Upanishads*, this process involves the formless and attributeless Brahma desiring to manifest multiple forms, thereby energizing the universe's emergence through the vibration of Consciousness.

In the *Upanishads*, *Brahma* is portrayed as formless and devoid of attributes (निर्गुण, निराकार). However, this representation may not resonate with the general public, who often seek a God with auspicious attributes. *Purănas* provide an alternative portrayal of God with positive attributes like kindness and forgiveness. There is no inherent conflict between these perspectives. In the *Bhagvad Gită*, *Lord Krishna* affirms, "In whatever form you worship Me, I strengthen your faith in that very form."

Within the *Purănas*, three main sects emerge: *Vaishnav*, *Shaiva*, and *Shăkta*. Let's explore the *Vaishnav* sect's account of the universe's creation. For *Vaishnavites*, Lord *Vishnu* serves as the universe's source. He is depicted as slumbering in the primordial ocean, from which a lotus sprouts from His navel, giving rise to *Brahmă*, the world's creator. This lotus symbolizes consciousness, while *Brahmă* embodies *Lord Vishnu's* creative power. *Brahmă* subsequently begets *Sarasvati*, the goddess of wisdom, and *Lakshmi*, *Lord Vishnu's* consort, symbolizing prosperity and abundance.

The aforementioned aspects of the *Purănas* primarily pertain to matters of faith and devotion. Faith occupies a distinct and significant place. It's crucial to recognise that not all sections of the *Purănas* are conducive to reasoning; they serve as supplementary texts designed for the common populace. Despite this, the *Purănas* remain highly beneficial and popular among general readers.

Even Western intellectuals who've delved into Upanishads and other Indian philosophical and cultural scriptures hold immense respect for Hinduism and India's heritage. Many globally renowned writers and thinkers, such as German scholar Max Muller, American authors Mark Twain and Will Durant, and French writer Romain Rolland, have expressed admiration for Hindu scriptures and Indian culture.

Now, it's astounding to encounter the words of a distinguished son of Mother India, the renowned writer *Aravind Adiga*. In his book 'White Tiger' (winner of 'The Man Booker Prize 2008'), he makes certain statements about India that warrant attention:

"Hindus have 360,000,000 gods... all the Muslims you meet are illiterate or covered head to toe in black burkas or looking for buildings to blow up."

Furthermore, he writes: *"I am an Indian faithful voter and yet have not seen the inside of the voting booth."*

The back cover carries the following statement: *"...an incisive work, relentless in its peeling back of the facade of 'India Rising' to expose its decaying core..."*

It's evident that the writer seeks to tarnish the image of Indian religion and democracy. Nonetheless, it's important to recognise that admiration for Indian religions resonates worldwide, and India is recognised as the world's largest democracy and the birthplace of democracy.

Criticism against Hindus regarding polytheism has existed since *Buddha's* time. The *Buddhist* text *'Bhikkhuni Samyutta'* mentions that Hindus have thirty-three (33) gods. Some might even claim Hindus have 33 *Koti* gods (Koti has two meanings - Type and Crore, which equals 10 million). The *Rigveda* references 209 gods. When comprehending the concepts of god and God, anything becomes possible.

As previously mentioned, when contradictions arise between Purănas and *Upanishads*, the *Upanishads* take precedence, as *Purănas* serve as secondary texts intended for the common populace. Through studying the *Upanishads*, one can deduce that *Sanătan Dharma* adheres to a monotheistic philosophy.

The *Gită* (13th chapter) elegantly captures the ineffable. Let's examine some examples:

"The Supreme Truth exists both outside and within all beings, animate and inanimate. Being subtle, He transcends the material senses' capacity to perceive. Despite being distant, He is close to all." - Gită 13.17

"Though the Supreme Soul appears divided among all beings, He is never divided. He remains undivided, sustaining every living entity. Understand that He engenders and engulfs all." - Gită 13.17

Similar *Slokas* can be found in the *Upanishads*, *Bhagvad Gită*, and authoritative scriptures like the *Brahmasutra*.

Now, let's explore what the *Upanishads* reveal about gods:

"यो देवानां प्रभवः च उद्भवः च विश्वाधिपः।"

Shvetăshvatara Upanishad 4/12
(Lord of the world who creates gods and increases their power...)

As stated in the above scripture and others like *Mundakopanishad* 2/1/7 and *Gită* 10/2, gods are created by God and are mortal like other beings.

"तस्मात् च देवाः बहुधा सम्प्रसूताः..."

Mundakopanishad 2/1/7

(By that (*Brahma*) several gods were created)

Regarding God, *Brahma* (ब्रह्म), the *Upanishads* assert that He is transcendental, the creator and protector of the entire creation, subtler than the subtlest, pervading all of creation and beyond. He can be known by a purified soul through His grace (*Ishăvasya Upanishad* 5, *Shvetăshvatara Upanishad* 3.20, *Kathopanishad* 1.2.20). By knowing Him, gods and *Rishis* attain peace and liberation from the cycle of death and birth. He is one but manifests in different forms.

The manifested energy of God, which is benevolent for humanity, such as the sun, fire, air, rivers, medicinal plants, etc., is revered as gods by emotionally inclined *Aryans*. In the *Rigveda*, many *Mantras* have been composed to adore mountains, rivers, plants, fire, etc.

However, the status of gods can be understood through a line in the *Gită* where *Lord Krishna* says:

"न मे विदुः सुरगणाः प्रभवं न महर्षयः।"

Gită 10/2

(Neither the gods nor the great sages know Me)

Even every human being is considered as a manifested God. Scriptures say:

"अहम् ब्रम्हास्मि, तत् त्वम् असि।"

(I am *Brahma*, and you are also the same.)

Even the Sufis share a similar opinion. *Jainism* also affirms that every soul is capable of attaining infinite consciousness, power, and bliss, inherent in its very nature. The lives of *Tirthankars* are exemplary in this regard, and Hindus recognise some *Tirthankars* as incarnations of *Vishnu*. They may also be considered as gods. Hindus are open in their belief, considering Bhagavăn Buddha as an incarnation of *Vishnu*, despite *Buddha's* lack of faith in *Vedas*, and *Buddhism* being recognised as a distinct religion.

According to *Buddhist* literature, during the process of attaining salvation, in the 7th stage, one becomes free from time and space and is able to merge with the infinite. However, out of compassion for all beings, he may take birth again.

The manifested energy of God, which is benevolent, is represented as gods. His earnest desire is to help the suffering people of the world.

Hindu scriptures state that mothers are gods, fathers and ancestors are gods, teachers are gods, and guests are gods.

मातृ देवो भव, पितृ देवो भव, गुरु देवो भव, अतिथि देवो भव

(All living and non-living entities deserving respect fall under the category of gods.)

Our ancestors, the *Rishis*, had communion with nature and the world, filled with love and respect, like clouds loaded with water ready to pour it in a suitable place. In the Rigveda, even a hand-glove has been considered as a god because it protected men from the sharp strings of bows.

There are intriguing examples of poetic sentiments and love of *Rishis* for gods in the hymns of *Vedas*: *"Hail Usha, daughter of the sky... Thou sweetly smilest, goddess fair, Disclosing all the youthful grace, Thy bosom bright, thy radiant face, And the luster of thy golden hair.... All eyes to fix, all hearts subject."*

Actually, the freedom to select a path according to convenience or mental and spiritual level is also one of the reasons for the existence of many gods. The Supreme Energy has also been categorized according to *Gunas*, attributes: *Sattva* (purity, harmony), *Rajas* (passion, motion), and *Tamas* (inertia, darkness). For wisdom, *Sarasvati*, a *Sătvik* deity, is prayed to, and for prosperity, *Lakshmi*, a *Răjasik* deity, is revered. However, when someone is setting out for a battlefield and may have to kill enemies, they may pray to *Kăli*, a *Tămasik* deity.

There is no harm in worshipping deities. The objective of worship or prayer is the calmness of mind and positive thoughts, which can be achieved through any prayer done with faith and reverence. *Lord Krishna says in the Gită (9/23): "Those who are devotees of other gods and worship them with faith, actually worship only Me, O son of Kunti, but their method is defective."*

The next important criticism is related to idolatry. Idol-worship has been particularly encouraged by *Purănas*, both in homes and temples, and is generally practiced by followers of *Bhakti*. A form of an image is necessary for worship in the beginning, as it serves as a symbol of God or deities, making the prayer or worship simpler. Idol-worship is not limited to Hindus; Christians worship the Cross, *Muslims* have the image of the *Kăba* in their minds during prayer, and *Buddhists* and *Jains* have idols of *Lord Buddha* and *Lord Mahăvira.*

Even *Yogis* meditate on some imaginable things like Om or some sound of *Mantra*, light, or sound. The mind needs a non-abstract symbol for meditation or prayer, and a symbol is necessary for fixing the fickle mind. No one can concentrate without a symbol in the beginning. Although the image is prayed to, the worshiper feels the presence of the deity and pours out devotion unto it. Faith is significant and possesses magical power. When a devotee sets out for a temple, he does not go to the idol but to his Lord, immersed in adoration even on the way to the temple. The divinity of the all-pervading Lord is vibrant in every atom, and idols serve as a means of easy communication.

Among several spiritual practices, *Yoga* is considered the best, and among various methods of *Yoga*, *Bhakti Yoga* is the easiest and simplest. *Bhakti Yoga* becomes more accessible and effective in the presence of an idol or presiding deity. Hence, idol-worship is very popular among Hindus.

Most Hindus have faith in idol-worship, and the results are self-evident. Many saints like *Tulsidăs* (devotee of *Lord Răma*), *Chaitanya Mahăprabhu*, *Narsi Mehta*, *Miră Băi*, *Rasakhan* (devotees of *Lord Krishna*), and many saints from the South and other regions attained God-realization starting from idol-worship. However, not everyone can be mystic saints like *Kabir*; it requires a different level and method.

The *Upanishads* state:

"न तस्य प्रतिमा अस्ति यस्य नाम महद्यशः।"

Svetăsvataropanisad 4/19

(There cannot be an idol of God or His parallel; His name is great.)

"आदिः स संयोगनिमित्तहेतुः परः त्रिकालात् अपि दृष्टः।
तं विश्वरूपं भवभूतमीड्यं देवं स्वचित्तस्थम् उपस्य पूर्वम्।"

Svetăsvataropanisad 6/5

(He; who is instrumental in combining *Prakriti* and *Purush*, the first cause, transcends time, manifests as the creation, present inside everyone; should be prayed.)

The worship of idols or images, unknown in the Vedic period, gradually dominated Hindu society later on. *Upanishads* advise the adore of formless all pervading of God. However, worship or prayer for the transcendental Supreme is not so easy.

In the *Gită*, *Lord Krishna* says (12/5):

"For those whose minds are attached to the unmanifested, impersonal feature of the Supreme, the advancement is difficult."

Maharshi Patanjali also advocates that the favorite deity (इष्टदेव) makes *Yoga* practice easier. (*Patanjali Yogasutra, Samădhipad 44)*

Actually, there are different stages of worship. The first is the worship of idols. Next is the recitation of *Mantras* and offering of prayers, then meditation on something conceivable, and lastly meditation on the transcendental or attributeless *Brahma*. A synthesis of all or many may be practiced. *Upanishads* talk about the transcendental *Brahma*, but during the performance of meditation, they also take the help of some imaginable symbol. The *Upanishads* advise meditating on *Om* or *Om*-chanting, the symbol of the formless *Brahma*.

तस्य वाचकः प्रणवः। पातंजलयोगप्रदीप, समाधिपाद 27

(His name is *Prarav*, Om)

ओम् इति ध्यायथ .. मुण्डकोपनिषद-2/2/6

(Meditate only on Om)

सुरत समानी शब्द में, ताहि काल न खाहि। कबीर

(When consciousness enters *Om*-chanting, one becomes immortal)

The objective of all the paths in Hinduism is the same. Followers of all the paths are respected by all. *Kabir* is a mystic; he was the disciple of *Swami Rămănanda*, who was a *Vaishnav* saint. *Swami Vivekănanda* did not follow idolatry, although he was a disciple of *Swami Rămakrishna Parămahansa*, who was a devotee of mother *Kăli* and an idol-worshipper. Therefore, there is no virtual difference between the paths. Paths are many; one can follow any in which he feels comfortable.

If idol-worship does not harm or hurt anybody, then why so much bitter criticism? There is a controversy about the Shiva *Linga*. *Linga* means symbol. The Hindu religion is very old. In the olden days, when it was not easy to keep the idols of deities, stone symbols were used for the purpose. It is still prevalent. Stone pieces are used as symbols of *Lord Shiva*, *Lord Vishnu*, and Divine Mothers. The stone symbol of *Lord Vishnu* is called *Shaligrăma*, and that of the Divine Mother is called *Pindi*.

Another common criticism is that *Lord Krishna* had more than 16,000 wives. The matter is also quoted from the *Purănas* without knowing the background. According to the *Purănas*, *Lord Krishna* defeated and killed *Bhaumăsura* or *Narkăsura*, the king of *Pragjyotishapur*, a *Himalayan* territory on the border of *Amarăvati*, the kingdom of *Aryan's* king *Indra*. *Bhaumăsura* defeated *Indra*, was wicked, oppressive, and cruel. He captured 16,100 virgins from different parts of the Indian peninsula and kept them in his harem. *Krishna* liberated them and brought them to *Dvărika* because they were helpless. After liberation, there was a great problem before them: how to get a livelihood, where to go, and who would accept them. *Krishna* married all of them to provide acceptance, sustainability, and respect they deserved as women. He made arrangements for their residence in a locality near *Dvărika*, and they were provided with all essentials for a happy life.

The caste system in Hinduism is also one of the main criticisms. Certainly, it is not appreciable. *Sanătan Dharma* is very old, and in any system, some impurities and anomalies may appear when it becomes very old. Originally, the caste system was quality-based during the *Vedic* period. It became hereditary during the post-*Vedic* period. The caste was based on the qualities and lifestyle of a person. The person with *Sătvik* tendency is Brahman, with *Răjasik* tendency is *Kshatriya*, and with *Tămasik* tendency is *Shudra*. *Brahman* originates from the *Sanskrit* root *'Bra,'* which means wide. *Brahman* means one with wide knowledge. In our scriptures, the word has been used for a learned person with wisdom and vast knowledge.

Brahman Scripture is a part of the *Veda*, which describes the method of Hindu rituals like *Yajna*. The persons with knowledge of this scripture were called *Brahman*. Even *Manusmriti*, which is criticized for the caste system, states:

"जन्मना जायते शूद्रः संस्कारेण द्विज उच्यते।"

(Everyone is *Shudra* by birth and after good foundation, *Sanskăr*, he is called *Dvija*.)

The upper three *Varnas*: *Brahmin*, *Kshatriya*, and *Vaishya*, are referred to as *Dvijas*. *Dvijas* are individuals who have undergone a second birth through qualification.

Manusmriti is also against the determination of caste by birth. *Manusmriti*, which is criticized for the caste system, holds the view that if a *Brahmin* is not learned and is solely engaged in ritualism for livelihood, they fall into the category of *Shudra* during their lifetime. (*Manusmriti* 171) Thus, according to *Manusmriti*, the caste system is not inherently hereditary. Originally, *Shudra* does not denote a specific caste, but rather a person who is illiterate, dull, and lethargic (with a *Tămasik* inclination). However, the upper three *Varnas* are privileged within the system. It is natural for them to favor a hereditary system. Nevertheless, despite the prevailing caste system, learned individuals are always respected regardless of their caste. *Vălmiki Rishi*, the author of *Rămăyăna*, was not born a *Brahmin*, yet he was a remarkable poet, philosopher, and *Guru*. He is esteemed in society as *Maharshi*. *Kabir* was a weaver, and *Raidăs* was a shoemaker; still, they are revered as great saints. Numerous other examples exist. Nonetheless, it cannot be denied that the flawed caste system still persists in Hinduism, although it is gradually diminishing. Sanătan Dharma is not a closed religion. Hindus are always willing to adapt.

I have been deeply distressed to hear an ugly criticism about *Brahmă* and goddess *Saraswati*. As I understand it, *Brahmă* (ब्रह्मा) represents a facet of the Supreme Energy that created the universe. Having already fashioned matter and energy, his work is nearly complete, except for the advancement of consciousness. Consciousness or wisdom is also a product of *Brahmă*, manifesting as Mother *Saraswati*, a deity venerated for wisdom. Thus, she is referred to as the daughter of *Brahmă*. Both are not bound by physical bodies. This statement carries symbolic meaning.

Similarly, *Lord Vishnu* and *Mahesh* share a similar narrative. *Vishnu* embodies the energy that sustains and safeguards the universe and is revered as the god of prosperity. *Mahesh* or *Shiva* embodies the aspect of Supreme Energy responsible for dissolution.

"The power to destroy is also the power to save." Consequently, *Shiva* embodies attributes of benevolence, forgiveness, kindness, and more. Shiva is Adiyogi, the first Yogi, *Vaidyanath* (the god of healers), *Pashupati*. A god with virtuous attributes fulfills the devotees' needs.

In the *Gită*, *Lord Krishna* affirms:

"I respond to my devotee in the same manner and intensity that the devotee desires." (Gită 4/11)

The origins of Shaivism can be traced back to the concept of *Rudra* in the Rigveda:

"O Rudra, do not harm the great or small among us, do not harm the growing boy, do not harm the mature man."
- Rigveda.

The benevolent characteristics of *Rudra* are emphasized in the renowned Satarudriya of the *Yajurveda*. The famous *Mahămrityunjaya Mantra*, from *Yajurveda* is the prayer of lord Shiva, for the protection from illness and untimely death.

In the *Gită*, *Krishna* states:

"Among the Rudras, I am Shankar or Shiva." (Gită 10.23)

Vaishnavism and *Shaivism* are two prominent sects within Hinduism. Both deities are revered by Hindus of all affiliations. My mother advised me to chant the name of *Lord Shiva* while taking medicines and the name of *Lord Vishnu* while donning new attire.

During the act of deity worship, a direct connection is established with our chosen deity (*Ishtadev*). This moment offers an opportunity to seek forgiveness and embark on a new life.

Above all, those who are scholarly and critical should adhere to the teachings of the *Upanishads* or *Bhagvad Gită*. As previously mentioned, *Sruti* (revealed scripture) takes precedence over *Smriti* (remembered scripture) when rational evidence is sought. The literary corpus of *Sanătan Dharma* is extensive and diverse due to the numerous thinkers and the freedom of expression. Logical analysis and skepticism are open to all, but they should be rooted in philosophical scriptures.

The *Upanishads* and *Gită* are structured in a question-and-answer format. The Brahmasutra begins with: 'अथ अतः ब्रह्मजिज्ञासा।' (Now let us commence the inquiry into *Brahmin*.)

Critics often draw material from *Purănaic* stories or epic narratives. *Purănas* are matters of faith, serving a purpose especially for the general populace. Combining history and mythology, *Purănas* offer spiritual and moral teachings through inspirational stories, exemplary characters, and illuminating discussions. They also deepen devotees' faith in their chosen deities.

I am deeply heartened when witnessing a crowd of women, particularly innocent, modest, and introverted homemakers, converging on the temple in adoration, to pour water over the *Shiva Lingam* (the symbolic representation of Lord Shiva) on the occasion of *Shiva Rătri* or during the month of Săvan (a Hindu month). This reveals that the *Purănas* hold greater popularity, utility, and moral significance for the common people compared to the profound philosophies of the *Upanishads*. Equally astonishing is news of scientists from ISRO seeking blessings from *Somanăth* (Lord of the Moon, Shiva) and *Lord Tirupati Bălăji* before launching *Chandrayăn-3* (the third lunar mission). This demonstrates the profound devotion and faith of rational scientists inspired by seemingly irrational Purănas.

As the saying goes:

'अष्टादश पुराणेषु व्यासस्य बचनद्वयम् ।
परोपकारः पुण्याय पापाय परपीडनम्।'

(Amidst the eighteen *Purănas*, recognise only two teachings of *Maharshi Vyăsa* as true - that helping others leads to virtue and harming others leads to sin.)

Certain Hindus criticize other Hindu sects to establish their own superiority. However, for philosophical discourse, only three authoritative texts (*Prasthănatrayi*) are considered valid: the *Upanishads*, *Gită*, and *Brahmasutra*. These texts elucidate the philosophical truths of the *Vedas*. True truth-seekers should strive to comprehend the essence of *Dharma* before engaging in criticism. The Srutis are profound and may not be easily comprehended by all. Hence, the *Purănas* have been crafted for the common populace. *Sanătan Dharma* is altruistic, humanistic, universal, noble, and open-minded in nature.

'सर्वत्र समबुद्धयः, ते प्राप्तवन्ति मामेव सर्वभूतहिते रताः। गीता 12/4

(One who maintains an impartial intellect towards all and is dedicated to the welfare of all beings, attains Me.)

Let us explore some comparăble noble thoughts from the *Vedas* and *Upanishads*.

'यस्तु सर्वाणि भूतानि आत्मनि एव अनुपस्यति।
सर्वभूतेषु च आत्मानं ततो न विजुगुप्सते।' ईशावास्योपनिषद, मंत्र 6

(One who perceives every being within the Self and the Self within every being, harbors no animosity.)

Across the various scriptures of *Sanătan Dharma*, whether Shruti or *Smriti*, *Upanishads* or *Purănas*, the *Rishis* consistently advise against any form of violence - be it mental, verbal, or physical. In some instances, they recommend the principle of 'like for like' or 'tit for tat,' particularly in treatises on governance like *Vidur Niti* or *Kautilya's Arthashăstra*, when dealing with those who intend harm.

Thousands of years ago, a *Rishi* implored:

'मनुर्भव - ऋग्वेद 10.53.6' (Be humane.)

Another *Rishi* prays:

'नय सुपथा राये अस्मान्। ऋग्वेद 1/189/1'

(Guide us on the righteous path towards prosperity.)

Dharma places its trust in the boundless potential of the soul, achievable through a pure soul, a tranquil and serene mind, and positive thoughts. *Sanătan Dharma* is universal and advocates collective well-being. It is a spiritual journey that centers on maintaining inner peace, regardless of the method chosen - prayer, idol worship, or various forms of *Yoga*. The greater the serenity of the mind, the closer one feels to the all-encompassing Cosmic Consciousness, the Supreme. His presence is felt as a guide, a protector, and the architect of one's destiny. Amidst a multitude of thinkers, scriptures, and choices, if there is a need for change, *Sanătan Dharma* is open and ever-ready to learn and elevate itself toward higher truths.

The world's oldest literature, the *Rigveda*, proclaims:

'आ नो भद्राः क्रतवो यन्तु विश्वतो अद्ब्धासो अपरितास उद्भिदः।
देवा नो तथासदभिद् वृधे असन्नाप्रायुवो रक्षितोरो दिवे दिवे।' ऋग्वेद 1/89/1

(May noble and auspicious thoughts come to us from all directions, uplifting us to a higher state. May the gods who protect us enhance our progress day by day.)

Notes

Notes